THE SCOTTISH AMERICANS

Consulting Editors

Ann Orlov
Managing Editor, Harvard
Encyclopedia of American
Ethnic Groups

M. Mark Stolarik
*President, The Balch Institute
for Ethnic Studies, Philadelphia*

Daniel Patrick Moynihan
*U.S. Senator from New York,
Senior Consulting Editor*

THE SCOTTISH AMERICANS

Catherine Aman

CHELSEA HOUSE PUBLISHERS

New York   Philadelphia

On the cover: Three sergeants of the 78th Highlanders, Royal Canadian Army.

CHELSEA HOUSE PUBLISHERS
Editor-in-Chief: Remmel Nunn
Managing Editor: Karyn Gullen Browne
Copy Chief: Juliann Barbato
Picture Editor: Adrian G. Allen
Art Director: Maria Epes
Deputy Copy Chief: Mark Rifkin
Assistant Art Director: Noreen Romano
Manufacturing Manager: Gerald Levine
Systems Manager: Lindsey Ottman
Production Manager: Joseph Romano
Production Coordinator: Marie Claire Cebrián

The Peoples of North America
Senior Editor: Kathy Kuhtz

Staff for THE SCOTTISH AMERICANS
Associate Editor: Scott Prentzas
Copy Editor: Brian Sookram
Picture Researcher: Melanie Sanford
Cover Illustration: Paul Biniasz
Banner Design: Hrana Janto

First Printing

1   3   5   7   9   8   6   4   2

Library of Congress Cataloging-in-Publication Data
Aman, Catherine.
   The Scottish Americans/Catherine Aman.
      p. cm.—(The Peoples of North America)
   Includes bibliographical references and index.
   ISBN 1-55546-132-8
         0-7910-0303-5 (pbk.)
   1. Scottish Americans—Juvenile literature. I. Title. II. Series.
E184.S3A42 1991   90-2400
973'.049163—dc20   CIP

CONTENTS

THE PEOPLES OF NORTH AMERICA

CHELSEA HOUSE PUBLISHERS

A NATION
OF NATIONS

Daniel Patrick Moynihan

The Constitution of the United States begins: "We the People of the United States . . ." Yet, as we know, the United States was not then and is not now made up of a single group of people. It is made up of many peoples. Immigrants and bondsmen from Europe, Asia, Africa, and Central and South America came here or were brought here, and still they come. They forged one nation and made it their own. More than 100 years ago, Walt Whitman expressed this great central fact of America: "Here is not merely a nation, but a teeming Nation of nations."

Although the ingenuity and acts of courage of these immigrants, our ancestors, shaped the North American way of life, we sometimes take their contributions for granted. This fine series, *The Peoples of North America*, examines the experiences and contributions of different immigrant groups and how these contributions determined the future of the United States and Canada.

Immigrants did not abandon their ethnic traditions when they reached the shores of North America. Each ethnic group had its own customs and traditions, and each brought different experiences, accomplishments, skills, values, styles of dress, and tastes in food that lingered long after its arrival. Yet this profusion of differences created a singularity, or bond, among the immigrants.

The United States and Canada are unusual in this respect. Whereas religious and ethnic differences have sparked intolerance throughout the rest of the world—from the 17th-century religious wars to the 19th-century nationalist movements in Europe to the near extermination of the Jewish people under Nazi Germany—North Americans have struggled to learn how to respect each other's differences and live in harmony.

Our two countries are hardly the only two in which different groups must learn to live together. There is no nation of significant size anywhere in the world which would not be classified as multi-ethnic. But only in North America are there so *many* different groups, most of them living cheek by jowl with one another.

This is not easy. Look around the world. And it has not always been easy for us. Witness the exclusion of Chinese immigrants, and for practical purposes Japanese also, in the late 19th century. But by the late 20th century, Chinese and Japanese Americans were the most successful of all the groups recorded by the census. We have had prejudice aplenty, but it has been resisted and recurrently overcome.

The remarkable ability of Americans to live together as one people was seriously threatened by the issue of slavery. Thousands of settlers from the British Isles had arrived in the colonies as indentured servants, agreeing to work for a specified number of years on farms or as apprentices in return for passage to America and room and board. When the first Africans arrived in the then-British colonies during the 17th century, some colonists thought that they too should be treated as indentured servants. Eventually, the question of whether the Africans should be treated as inden-tured, like the English, or as slaves who could be owned for life was considered in a Maryland court. The court's calamitous decree held that blacks were slaves bound to a lifelong servitude, and so also were their children. America went through a time of moral ex-amination and civil war before it finally freed African slaves and their descendants. The principle that all people are created equal had faced its greatest challenge and survived.

Yet the court ruling that set blacks apart from other races fanned flames of discrimination that burned long after slavery was abolished—and that still flicker today. Indeed, it was about the time of the American Civil War that European theories of evolution were turned to the service of ranking different peoples by their presumed distance from our apelike ancestors.

When the Irish flooded American cities to escape the famine in Ireland, the cartoonists caricatured the typical "Paddy" (a common term for Irish immigrants) as an apelike creature with jutting jaw and sloping forehead.

By the 20th century, racism and ethnic prejudice had given rise to virulent theories of a Northern European master race. When Adolf Hitler came to power in Germany in 1933, he popularized the notion of an Aryan race. Only a man of the deepest ignorance and evil could have done this. *Aryan* is a Sanskrit word, which is to say the ancient script of what we now think of as India. It means "noble" and was adopted by linguists—notably by a fine German scholar, Max Müller—to denote the Indo-European family of languages. Müller was horrified that anyone could think of it in terms of race, especially a race of blond-haired, blue-eyed Teutons. But the Nazis embraced the notion of a master race. Anyone with darker and heavier features was considered inferior. Buttressed by these theories, the German Nazi state from 1933 to 1945 set out to destroy European Jews, along with Poles, Gypsies, Russians, and other groups considered inferior. It nearly succeeded. Millions of these people were murdered.

The tragedies brought on by ethnic and racial intolerance throughout the world demonstrate the importance of North America's efforts to create a society free of prejudice and inequality.

A relatively recent example of the New World's desire to resolve ethnic friction nonviolently is the solution that the Canadians found to a conflict between two ethnic groups. A long-standing dispute as to whether Canadian culture was properly English or French resurfaced in the mid-1960s, dividing the peoples of the French-speaking Province of Quebec from those of the English-speaking provinces. Relations grew tense, then bitter, then violent. The Royal Commission on Bilingualism and Biculturalism was established to study the growing crisis and to propose measures to ease the tensions. As a result of the commission's recommendations, all official documents and statements from the national government's capital at Ottawa are now issued in both French and English, and bilingual education is encouraged.

The year 1980 marked a coming of age for the United States's ethnic heritage. For the first time, the U.S. Bureau of the Census asked people about their ethnic background. Americans chose from more than 100 groups, including French Basque, Spanish Basque, French Canadian, African-American, Peruvian, Armenian, Chinese, and Japanese. The ethnic group with the largest response was English (49.6 million). More than 100 million Americans claimed ancestors from the British Isles, which includes England, Ireland, Wales, and Scotland. There were almost as many Germans (49.2 million) as English. The Irish-American population (40.2 million) was third, but the next-largest ethnic group, the African-Americans, was a distant fourth (21 million). There was a sizable group of French ancestry (13 million) as well as of Italian (12 million). Poles, Dutch, Swedes, Norwegians, and Russians followed. These groups, and other smaller ones, represent the wondrous profusion of ethnic influences in North America.

Canada too has learned more about the diversity of its population. Studies conducted during the French/English conflict showed that Canadians were descended from Ukrainians, Germans, Italians, Chinese, Japanese, native Indians, and Inuit, among others. Canada found it had no ethnic majority, although nearly half of its immigrant population had come from the British Isles. Canada, like the United States, is a land of immigrants for whom mutual tolerance is a matter of reason as well as principle. But note how difficult this can be in practice, even for persons of manifest goodwill.

The people of North America are the descendants of one of the greatest migrations in history. And that migration is not over.

Koreans, Vietnamese, Nicaraguans, Cubans, and many others are heading for the shores of North America in large numbers. This mix of cultures shapes every aspect of our lives. To understand ourselves, we must know something about our diverse ethnic ancestry. Nothing so defines the North American nations as the motto on the Great Seal of the United States: *E Pluribus Unum*—Out of Many, One.

The Croil family pauses alongside its luggage at the end of their journey from Scotland to Canada in 1888. Scottish immigrants first arrived in North America in the beginning of the 17th century, and nearly 1.5 million Scots have immigrated to the continent over the last 4 centuries.

THE SCOTS IN NORTH AMERICA

Scottish immigration to North America began in the early colonial era and has continued ever since. The first Scot in the New World was probably Thomas Henderson, who came to Virginia with the earliest British settlers during the first decade of the 17th century. Since then, nearly 1.5 million Scots have followed his path. In the United States today, more than 10 million people claim some Scottish heritage, and more than 142,000 have solely Scottish ancestry. Although the Scots are an almost entirely assimilated group in North America, many hints remain of their significant role in the histories of both the United States and Canada.

The historian Marcus Lee Hansen has noted that immigrants tend to cling to the institutions and customs that they are able to bring with them from their homeland. Leaving behind all that they are familiar with to come to a foreign country makes them cherish and sometimes magnify their old practices as a source of identity. Today, North Americans of Scottish descent remain proud of their cultural heritage, even if they are only partly Scottish or have lived in North America for many generations. Habit, nostalgia, and pride keep alive a number of customs and events. For instance, Scottish games are held throughout the continent. These outdoor festivals include entertainment, such as Highland dancing, and traditional contests of strength and skill such as the caber toss in which contestants throw a tree trunk (caber) the size of a telephone pole.

Some Scottish Americans celebrate their cultural heritage with the annual observance of poet Robert Burns's birthday on January 25. These festivities, organized by Burns Clubs across the country, usually include the reading of the Scottish poet's works, drinking scotch, and eating haggis (a traditional Scottish dish consisting of sheep organs, onions, and seasonings boiled and served in a sheep's stomach).

One way that Scottish immigrants commemorated their origins was to transplant place-names from Scotland to the New World. The incidence of Scottish place-names in North America indicates the influence and wide distribution of the immigrants. The United States alone boasts eight Aberdeens, eight Edinburghs, seven Glasgows, and eight places merely called Scotland outright. Many towns are named after the great clans— Campbell (10), Cameron (16), Crawford (30), and Douglas (9)—some of which are also place-names in Scotland. A glance at the map also shows hundreds of place-names beginning with the common Scottish surname construction "Mc" or "Mac"; there are 130 in North Carolina alone. Throughout the Carolinas and Virginia, there are places that bear the names New Scotland, Caledonia, or Scotchtown.

One of the effects of immigrant nostalgia is the perpetuation of customs in the New World that have long since become outmoded in the homeland. For instance, the infatuation of Scottish Americans with clan tartans (woolen fabrics with plaid designs) has no basis in the contemporary political or social realities of Scotland. The clan system was permanently destroyed with the Scots' defeat at Culloden in 1746, and modern plaids are mostly inaccurate reconstructions created during the Victorian period.

Another manifestation of the continuing pride of Scottish Americans in their ancestry is the number of Scottish-American clubs and societies in North America. For example, there are independent clubs in a number of different cities that all have the name St. Andrew's Society, after the patron saint of Scotland. Most were chartered in the mid-18th century to provide financial assistance to poor Scottish immigrants and to help them find jobs. Although few destitute Scots immigrate to North America now, the clubs have endured as prestigious organizations with exclusive memberships. In fact, throughout the United States and Canada there are approximately 300 St. Andrew's Societies, Caledonian Clubs, and other Scottish societies. Additionally, there are more than 200 clan societies, which hold massive gatherings for all those who have the same Scottish surname.

Some of the customs the Scots brought to North America are now so thoroughly a part of the continent's

This late-19th-century composite photograph shows the past presidents of the Caledonian Society of Montreal. Scottish Americans preserve their heritage by remaining active in chapters of Scottish-American clubs such as the Caledonian Society.

Scottish immigrants compete in a curling match on the St. Lawrence River in 1878. Several facets of popular culture in North America originated in Scotland, including curling and golf.

culture that their source has been virtually forgotten. Golfing, for example, is a Scottish sport that is now a mainstay of North American leisure time, and curling, a Scottish ice game, is quite popular in Canada. The Caledonian Games, great athletic tournaments that were held in Scotland, were brought to the United States and eventually became the modern track and field events. It is, of course, impossible to forget the origins of Scotch whiskey.

In Scotland, the "kirk," or church, played a central role in everyday life. The church was the seat of moral authority and education, and it exerted tremendous influence in matters of civil authority as well. The Scots brought their principal religion, Presbyterianism, with them to the New World, where it continued to play a major part in their life. With 3 million members, the Presbyterian church is now one of the largest mainstream Protestant churches in the United States. In Canada, many members of the Presbyterian church joined with 2 other churches in 1925 to form the United Church of Canada, which numbered about 850,000 members in 1990. Today, the Presbyterian church in Canada is composed of those who did not assent to the union, and it has approximately 157,000 members.

The greatest contribution of Scotland to North America, however, was not the Scottish customs and pastimes transplanted here. It was the hardy immigrants themselves. They were strong, courageous, and stubborn. As a group, they were characterized as industrious, pragmatic, frugal, clannish, and reserved. Many Scottish immigrants came from tenant farms where the harsh climate and topography made farming a struggle. These conditions bred a respect for hard work and a certain severity of temperament, traits compounded by the Scots' Presbyterian faith. As Presbyterians, they believed that religion was a serious, personal responsibility, and they valued education so that all might be able to read the Bible. Immigrants with such traits are valuable to growing nations, and the Scottish role in building the United States and Canada should not be underestimated.

Among the people of Scottish ancestry who came to the New World are three distinct groups: the Lowland Scots, the Highland Scots, and the Scotch-Irish. Each group had its own motives for migration and its own experience in North America. The group known as the Scotch-Irish first emigrated from Scotland to Ireland. In the 17th century, the British, who were trying to subdue the Irish, encouraged Protestants from southern Scotland to settle on the captured lands of Irish Catholics. Thousands of Scots migrated to Northern Ireland, and many stayed for several generations. They lived there, however, in a state of perpetual and often bloody conflict with the Irish Catholics. Many ultimately left for North America in the late 18th and early 19th centuries. Because they had lived in Ireland for several generations before coming to the New World, their experiences were very different from those who came directly from Scotland. This book will not address the experiences of the Scotch-Irish—that requires an entire book of its own. It will instead look at the experiences of the Highland and Lowland Scots.

THE HOMELAND: ITS HISTORY AND PEOPLE

The people who left Scotland were indelibly stamped by its unique geography and history. Because the rigors of life in Scotland shaped the values and customs that Scottish immigrants brought with them to North America, it is necessary to understand Scotland and its long history in order to grasp the Scottish-American experience fully.

Geography

The distinguished 20th-century Scottish historian J. D. Mackie has noted that with only a knowledge of Scotland's geography one could guess the main features of its history. Indeed, the country's location and terrain have profoundly influenced the course of its development and the character of its people. Two factors are of

Near Glencoe, majestic hills over-look one of Scotland's few lush glens (valleys). Craggy mountains and small hills dominate much of Scotland's landscape, which has had a tremendous impact on the political and social life of its people. Because only one-fifth of Scotland is suitable for farming, many Scots have emigrated in search of better economic opportunities.

great historical importance in the location of Scotland: its distance from Europe and its proximity to England.

Scotland occupies the northern third of the island of Great Britain, which is one of a group of islands situated off the northwestern coast of Europe. For centuries, Scotland remained outside the mainstream of European civilization. Christianity and important historical movements, such as the Renaissance and the Reformation, reached the country relatively late and with less impact than they had on other European countries. More important, however, these forces reached and enriched Scotland's mighty neighbor, England, first. Throughout much of its history, Scotland was one of two kingdoms on a single island, and it was natural that the two powers long fought for dominance. England was always the stronger of the two countries economically and militarily, and the Scots' nationalism and pride were forged in stubborn resistance to conquest by their more powerful southern neighbor.

The total area of Scotland is 30,414 square miles (78,772 square kilometers). In comparison, England and Wales occupy 58,349 square miles (151,123 square kilometers). More than a tenth of Scotland's land area is in the remote, scattered islands of the Hebrides (500 islands) and the archipelagoes of Orkney and Shetland (together about 150 islands), which lie north and west of the mainland in the Atlantic Ocean and the North Sea. Whereas England is made up of gently rolling hills ideal for agriculture, craggy hills and mountains dominate Scotland's landscape. Only one-fifth of this barren land is suitable for farming, and only in the limited fertile areas of the southeast has agriculture ever been very profitable. English author and lexicographer Samuel Johnson (1709–84) once described the harshness of Scotland's terrain to a Scottish noble:

> Your country consists of two things, stone and water. There is, indeed, a little earth above the stone in some places, but a very little; and the stone is always appearing. It is like a man in rags; the naked skin is still peeping out.

The People

Who were the people who settled in this remote, inhospitable place? The early population of Scotland was composed of four peoples: the Picts, the Scots, the Britons, and the Angles. The Picts, the earliest inhabitants, occupied northern and northeastern Scotland. Themselves an amalgam of peoples, the Pict groups spoke several Celtic languages. The Scots, who spoke Gaelic, came from Northern Ireland across the southern islands of the Hebrides in the late 5th century, bringing with them an early form of Christianity. (Legend holds that Fergus, the leader of the first Scots settlement, brought with him the famous Stone of Destiny upon

Shaggy cattle, a familiar sight in the Highlands, graze along the shores of Loch Etive in Argyllshire. The economy of the Highlands has long been based on cattle and sheep raising and small-scale farming.

which all Scottish kings were crowned. The stone, which was moved to Scone in 838 and renamed the Stone of Scone, became a symbol of the Scottish monarchy; it was said that "wherever the stone should rest a King of Scots would reign.") The Britons, who inhabited the Lowlands, were part of the Roman-Celtic culture remaining after the Romans left Great Britain. The Angles were a Germanic people whose kingdom in the north of England was called Northumbria. They eventually merged with two other tribes—the Saxons and the Jutes—to form the Anglo-Saxon group.

The Highlands and the Lowlands

Scotland has always been divided geographically and culturally into the Highlands and the Lowlands. The Highlands, in the center and west of the country, are dominated by mountains interspersed with deep valleys called glens. The weather is typically damp and windy, and the land is mostly bleak and barren. Only the lower slopes are suitable for grazing and small-scale farming. This rugged topography made transport and communication difficult and tended to separate the population into self-sufficient groups, each occupying a valley and owing their allegiance to their kin.

Highlanders have always had a reputation for being fierce warriors. The stormy climate and lack of natural resources of their environment motivated them to plunder the wealth of others. The racial heritage of the Highlander is almost purely Celtic, and the fact that the Highlanders spoke Gaelic tended to isolate them further from the rest of the country. (In the more remote islands, Gaelic remains the primary language of many of the inhabitants.) Isolated and self-sufficient, the Highlanders resisted submitting to a single Scottish king. Their fierceness and independence, however, also made them a formidable force against outside invasion, which helped the nation grow.

The Lowland plains, located in the south and east of the country, has a climate and terrain better suited to farming. Although the preindustrial economy of the Highlands was mostly pastoral (sheep and cattle farming), that of the Lowlands was agricultural. With the advent of coal, iron, and steel production, the Lowlands became increasingly industrialized and urban. The Lowlanders have long been characterized as tough and enterprising people. Of mixed racial heritage, the Lowlanders have spoken English for centuries.

From early times, the basis of Scottish society was the kinship group known as the clan. Members of a clan had the same surname and were loyal to a chief who was the head of the clan. For instance, members of the clan Donald would all have the last name MacDonald. The Gaelic word *clann* means children, but not all members of a clan were descendants of the chief's ancestor, and eventually not all in a large clan took the name of its chief. Clans persisted through the Middle Ages in the Lowlands but were far more entrenched in the Highlands, where they continued to be a political force well into the 18th century. That kinship was as important as rank—if not more so—made the Scots an unpretentious people, a trait that they brought with them to North America.

History

Scotland's history is a long tale of resistance to invasion and subjugation. The Romans were the first to invade and occupy Scotland, from A.D. 80 to 110 and again from 140 to 180. In 120, they began building Hadrian's Wall—a massive, fortified barricade that extended from the Tyne River to Solway firth—much of which still stands. Unable to subdue the tribes to the north, the Roman emperor Hadrian had the wall built to mark and protect the northern boundary of the Roman Empire. Though the tribes eventually became Roman allies, even the wall failed to keep out the fierce raiding Picts.

The next great force to enter Scotland was Christianity. Saint Ninian began his conversions in 400, but it was the Irish missionary Saint Columba who success-

A scene etched on Trajan's Column in Rome shows legionnaires constructing Hadrian's Wall, a barricade stretching from Solway firth to the mouth of the Tyne River. Emperor Hadrian had the wall built in A.D. 120 to prevent Scottish raiders from invading Britain, then part of the Roman Empire.

fully converted the Picts in the late 6th century. During this time, the Scots, Picts, Britons, and Angles were warring among themselves, alternately allying against each other. The Picts were the strongest of the four groups militarily, but the Scots were animated by their Christianity. United in Christianity by Saint Columba, the Scots and the Picts were brought together politically under King Kenneth MacAlpin, a Scot who was crowned at Scone in 843. The consolidated kingdom came to be known as Scotia. Though differences between the Highlanders and the Lowlanders persisted—mirroring the different ethnic heritages of the two areas—eventually the four original peoples coalesced into one nation. Factors that contributed to their unification were their shared faith and the need to join together to resist outside aggressors.

The Danes presented a potent threat to the nascent kingdom. They invaded and occupied Shetland, Orkney, the Hebrides, and the northwest mainland. The Danes held on until 1266, enriching the racial mixture of northernmost Scotland. Internal forces could also be a threat. Moray, located in the north, was a particularly strong and independent region in the Highlands. In 1034, its chief, Macbeth, seized the throne after killing King Duncan I. Macbeth—whose actions provided the basis for Shakespeare's play—ruled until he was slain in 1057 by Duncan's son, Malcolm. Malcolm, who had spent his years of exile in England, brought many British ways to Scotland, including Norman-style feudalism under which lords and chiefs obtained land from the king in exchange for military service. During the 12th and 13th centuries, Scotland prospered and experienced a "golden age" of economic and cultural growth.

This long period of success and security came to an end with the death of the child-queen Margaret, the last heir of the House of Canmore. Despite her age, she had been betrothed to the son of the British king, Edward I. The British now had a legitimate claim to the Scottish throne. To avoid warfare, Edward put John de Baliol on the Scottish throne in 1292, forcing him first to swear to British authority. Changing his mind, Baliol attempted to throw off British authority. In the course of a bloody defeat, the Stone of Scone was taken by Edward I to Britain, never to be returned to Scotland.

Irish missionary Saint Columba (521–597) preaches to a group of Picts. In A.D. *563, Columba established a monastery off the Scottish coast on the island of Iona, which became the base from which he Christianized the Scottish mainland.*

Robert the Bruce (1274–1329) was crowned Robert I of Scotland in 1306 but had to wrest control of his kingdom from the British. After many setbacks, Robert I's forces recaptured most of Scotland, forcing King Edward III to recognize Scottish independence in 1327.

The stone became part of Edward's coronation throne, which still stands in Westminster Abbey in London.

Scotland was liberated from the British by Robert I, known as Robert the Bruce, who ruled from 1306 to 1329. He defeated the British army decisively at Bannockburn in 1314, the worst blow they were ever to suffer on Scottish soil. Britain attempted to employ papal authority to stake its claim against Bruce, using the threat of excommunication against him. The Scottish nobles and clergy replied to the pope with a stirring proclamation of their independence, known as the Declaration of Arbroath (1320), which concludes as follows:

> For as long as one hundred of us shall remain alive we shall never in any wise consent to submit to the rule of the English, for it is not for glory we fight, for riches, or for honors, but for freedom alone, which no good man loses but with his life.

The Scottish thirst for freedom eventually prevailed. In 1328 the British officially acknowledged King Robert, and in 1329 the pope recognized the full sovereignty of the Scottish kingdom.

Despite its newly regained independence, Scotland continued to experience hardships. Wars with Britain were a constant possibility and often a reality. These frequent conflicts with a more powerful nation impoverished Scotland. To balance the antagonism with Britain, Scotland often allied with France. Although culturally valuable, this alliance led Scotland into some disastrous and costly military conflicts. Scotland also experienced prolonged misfortune in its monarchy, with a string of infant monarchs and aged and ineffectual kings. Internal stability was threatened by bitter rivalry between the Crown and the nobility (chiefs and barons), which—along with the Catholic church—had gained tremendous wealth and power.

The reign of James IV (1488–1513) brought a respite from these national woes. His rule and that of his son,

James V (1513–42), brought the Renaissance to Scotland and guided progress in the economic, administrative, and social realms. Unfortunately, the "Auld Alliance" with France forced James IV into invading Britain. He was killed when his forces were crushed at Flodden in 1513.

Despite the high cost of allying with the French—and despite his subjects' growing distaste for Roman Catholicism—James V renewed ties with France. A wave of disillusionment with the wealth and abuses of the Roman Catholic church was sweeping through Europe, resulting in a powerful movement known as the Reformation, which called for changes in Christian institutions. In Britain, the Reformation allowed Henry VIII to break all ties with the Roman Catholic church and the pope. New churches, called Protestant churches, were formed in protest against the abuses of the Roman Catholic church. Because the Reformation and Protestantism were beginning to take hold in Scotland too, many felt the country should ally with Britain and not with France, which was Roman Catholic. Instead, James V married a daughter of the French king to cement his alliance with France. Though she lived only a short time, his second wife—Mary of Guise—was also French.

James V was a popular king who oversaw parliamentary and judicial improvements. It was his tie to France and the old religion, however, that eventually drew Scotland into conflict with Britain, culminating in a bloody defeat at Solway Moss in 1542. On his deathbed shortly thereafter, James received the news that Mary had given birth to a daughter. "It came with a lass, and it will pass with a lass," he said, recalling the year 1286 when the only heir was the infant girl Margaret, who was forced to marry a British prince. Her death had brought the end of a dynasty and subjugation to England. James's prophecy proved false. Mary, his daughter, would live a fascinating life, never submitting to marrying a British heir.

James V (1512–42) ascended to the Scottish throne in 1513 but did not assume control of his kingdom until he reached his 16th birthday in 1528. James instituted many laws that protected his subjects from the abuses of Scottish nobles. He took up arms against his uncle, King Henry VIII of Great Britain, but his forces were crushed at Solway Moss in 1542.

When Mary of Guise refused to have her infant daughter, Mary Stuart, betrothed to Edward VI, British forces invaded Scotland. Young Mary was sent to be raised in France and was promised to the dauphin, the eldest son of the king of France. Before she was 20 years old, she would marry, watch her young husband become king, and be widowed. In France, she was known as Mary, Queen of Scots. In 1561, still a teenager, she returned to rule the country of her birth.

In Mary's absence, the Scots had rebelled against political ties to France and religious ties to Rome. They were alarmed at the prospect of being governed by outsiders and angry at the tremendous wealth that the Roman Catholic church controlled. In 1557, the first Covenant, a declaration of religious freedom, was signed. Two years later, John Knox, a religious reformer, returned from Geneva to spearhead the growing rebellion. When Mary arrived, she found the reformers in control. The Treaty of Leith (1560) had renounced French involvement in and control of Scotland.

Queen Mary, though a Roman Catholic herself, was not initially hostile to the Protestants. Soon, however, she wed her cousin, Lord Darnley, a Roman Catholic and—like herself—a claimant to the British throne. Together they posed a threat to the Protestants in Scotland and Britain. Mary gave birth to a son, James, and shortly thereafter her husband was murdered. Mary, a fiercely independent woman, almost immediately mar-

Following the death of her husband, King Francis II of France, Mary Stuart (1542–87)—known popularly as Mary, Queen of Scots—returns to Edinburgh to rule the country of her birth. After marrying one of the alleged conspirators in the murder of her second husband, Mary lost the support of the Scottish nobles and was forced to abdicate. After fleeing to Great Britain, she was executed for her purported role in a Catholic plot against the life of Queen Elizabeth I.

ried the Earl of Bothwell, who was believed to be one of Darnley's killers. This act lost her the support of her subjects, and she was deposed in 1567 in favor of her infant son, James VI. In 1568 Mary fled to Britain and the dubious protection of Queen Elizabeth I. Mary was held prisoner, and her execution was finally ordered by Elizabeth in 1587.

During James VI's minority, conflict raged between Roman Catholics (supported by Europe) and Protestants. Within the Reformed church, a faction emerged that demanded the abolishment of the office of bishop and the end of royal authority in the governance of the church. This group became known as Presbyterians because they believed the church should be run by *presbyteries*, committees of ordinary ministers. The Presbyterians were stern and suspicious of religious hierarchies such as those found in the Roman Catholic church. In the remote northern Highlands opinion remained conservative, and Presbyterianism did not take hold as it did in the Lowlands.

Surrounded by conflicting religious factions, James became a shrewd and pragmatic leader. Realizing his dependence on the Presbyterians' support, he agreed to the formal establishment of their system in 1592, only to revoke his support two years later when the last of the rebellions by the Roman Catholics was put down. Though he reestablished his control of the church, he wisely realized how important the Scots' manner of worship had become to them. James VI ascended to the throne of England as James I in 1603. He was crowned on the Stone of Scone in Westminster Abbey, thereby fulfilling its ancient prophecy. He did not impose the British form of worship on the Scots. Given the range of religious opinion in Scotland, James's decision not to decree a universal form of worship was wise indeed.

James's son, Charles I, was not as politically adept as his father. Attempting to impose Anglicanism (the British form of Protestantism that established hierarchical offices such as bishoprics and made the king the

James I (1566–1625), son of Mary, Queen of Scots, sits upon the British throne. He ruled effectively in Scotland as James VI for 20 years before ascending to the British throne when Queen Elizabeth I died in 1603.

head of the church), he provoked the Scots into issuing the National Covenant (1638), which asserted their right to Presbyterianism. Though unwilling to concede this, Charles, who was losing the support of his people, could not muster the military strength to enforce his will. The Scots invaded and occupied northern Britain. At the outbreak of the English civil war, they pledged their support to the British Parliament in their fight against Charles.

The war ended with Puritan cavalry commander Oliver Cromwell in power, and many of the Covenanters who had supported Parliament decided to fight for the Restoration of the Stuart line—Charles I and then Charles II, after his father's execution—rather than submit to Cromwell. In retaliation, Cromwell invaded and defeated the Scots at Dunbar (1650) and at Worcester (1651). Under Cromwell, Scotland was politically and economically united with Britain, sharing in its Parliament and in its commercial markets.

The restoration of the Stuart monarchy in 1660 was generally accepted, although some Presbyterians resisted because James VII (James II of Great Britain), the second son of Charles I, was a Roman Catholic. James VII, however, decreed toleration of the Presbyterians, undermining the church hierarchy established by his predecessors. His use of royal prerogative was unacceptable to the English Parliament, which eventually drove him out in 1688 (the Glorious Revolution). James was supplanted by William of Orange, who, because he needed the Presbyterians' support, finally established the Presbyterian system in 1690. Highlanders loyal to James were horribly defeated in the Massacre of Glencoe in 1692.

The years since the reign of James VII had been prosperous ones with cultural achievements and great commercial development. Scottish colonies were founded in North America: in Nova Scotia, east New Jersey, and South Carolina. Free trade with Britain and its markets, however, stopped after the Restoration. Without support from Britain, a Scottish colony in Panama failed miserably. Economic friction between the two nations finally led to a treaty of union in 1707. Scotland surrendered political independence but gained the valuable right to English trade as well as the assurance that it would forever retain its own church, laws, and judicial system.

Armed resistance to the unification cropped up from time to time. For the most part, such resistance reflected

the sentiments of disaffected Roman Catholics, Episcopalians, and marginalized, clannish Highlanders in search of plunder. For all their romance, the famous Jacobite uprisings of 1715 and 1745 were hardly national movements. The Jacobites (derived from *Jacobus*, the Latin word for James) originally supported James VII after he was deposed and later sought to restore the Stuarts to the throne. When Charles Edward, the Young Pretender, was defeated at Culloden in 1746, the Stuart cause was forever crushed. The clan system was dealt a terrible blow as well; even wearing kilts and playing bagpipes was banned. The Highlanders were disarmed, and the landowning chiefs lost their political, military, and judicial authority. The Lowlanders were pleased by the defeat of the Highlanders, and disaffection with the English union finally ended. After 1746, Scotland forever ceased being an independent and distinct political entity.

Fighting on the side of Prince Charles Edward Stuart, the Young Pretender, in the second Jacobite uprising, Highland clansmen meet their doom at the Battle of Culloden in 1746. As a result of this failed attempt to restore the descendants of James I to the British throne, the clan system collapsed because Highland chiefs were forced to forfeit their ancestral authority.

James Blair (1656–1743), who moved from Scotland to the colonies in 1685, was the first president of the College of William and Mary. During the 17th and 18th centuries, many Scottish immigrants—a group that included a substantial number of educators, doctors, merchants, and statesmen—were influential in colonial society.

EARLY IMMIGRANTS: AN INFLUENTIAL MINORITY

Scotland was never a wealthy nation. Opportunities were limited and, particularly in the Highlands, eking an existence out of the land was a difficult business. In a letter written in 1772, Benjamin Franklin described the plight of the Scottish in this way:

> I have lately made a Tour thro' Ireland & Scotland. In those Countries a small Part of the Society are Landlords, great Noblemen, and Gentl[e]men, extremely opulent, living in the highest Affluence and Magnificence; the Bulk of the People Tenants, extremely poor, living in the most sordid Wretched-ness, in dirty Hovels of Mud and Straw, clothed only in Rags. . . .

Scottish financier and economist John Law (1671–1729) served as the minister of finance to King Louis XV of France. Beginning in the Middle Ages, many talented and ambitious Scots like Law left behind the economic limitations of their homeland in search of better prospects abroad, particularly in Europe.

Had I never been in the American Colonies, but was to form my Judgement of Civil Society by what I have lately seen, I should never advise a Nation of Savages to admit of Civilization; For I assure you; that, in Possession & Enjoyment of the various Comforts of Life, compar'd to the[se] People every [American] Indian is a Gentleman: And the Effect of this kind of Civil Society seems only to be, the depressing [of the] Multitudes below the Savage State that a few may be rais'd above it. . . .

Wanting to make the point that everyone was equal in the colonies, Franklin probably exaggerated the degree of economic inequality in Scotland. Compared with the English, the fortunes of Scottish nobles were quite modest. The fundamental truth, however, was that for much of its history, most of Scotland was remote and poor. For centuries, enterprising Scots had left home in search of greater opportunities elsewhere. Because Scots had a long tradition of migrating to other places, emigration to North America started slowly.

Throughout the Middle Ages, Scots traveled widely as religious pilgrims, scholars, and merchants. By 1650, some 50,000 Scots had settled in Ireland (the ancestors of the Scotch-Irish who later came to North America). The Scots also had a well-established tradition of entering into the service of foreign armies, and European wars provided ample chances for enterprising Scots to advance in the military. Scots were scattered throughout northern Europe, and many achieved great success in other nations. John Law became minister of finance to French king Louis XV; Earl Marischal Keith was an adviser of Frederick the Great of Prussia, and admirals Patrick Gordon and Samuel Greig served Russian czars. Queen Elizabeth I, Russian czar Peter the Great, Empress Catherine II, and Emperor Alexander I all had personal physicians who were Scottish, and other Scottish doctors ran hospitals from London to Moscow.

Although opportunities might be limited at home, the possibility of success in Europe discouraged Scots from undertaking the arduous move to North America.

Motivations for Migration

The earliest movement to the Americas came with the founding of Scottish colonies there. A short-lived colony was founded in Nova Scotia, Canada, in 1629. Religious persecution was the impetus for the founding of colonies at East Jersey (what is now eastern and northern New Jersey) in 1683 and South Carolina in 1684—the former a refuge for Quakers and the latter for Presbyterians. A settlement called New Caledonia was founded near Panama in 1698. None of these ventures succeeded, and most Scottish artisans and laborers were unwilling to migrate because better opportunities were available in Europe.

Some of those who left for North America went involuntarily. The deportation of criminals and rebels to distant places, known as transportation, was a long-standing practice. The Scottish government began transporting criminals and religious dissenters as early as the mid-17th century. The British government also transported Scottish rebels. In the years between 1648 and 1651, when the Scottish suffered three defeats at the hands of Cromwell, each loss resulted in several hundred Scots being transported to the New World. Similarly, in 1715 and 1745, more than 1,400 defeated Jacobite rebels were shipped off to North America.

Voluntary migration to the Americas had become more common by the end of the 17th century. The Union of Parliaments in 1707 facilitated trade between Scotland and the colonies and thus encouraged the emigration of merchants. Many went to Virginia, where the thriving tobacco industry provided many opportunities. As the rule of law extended over Scotland, armed raids by Highlanders against Lowlanders became less and less frequent. Without this additional source of income, the Highlanders began to find their

RESIDENT CHIEFS.

SCOTTISH GAMES AT JONES WOOD

Highland chiefs fraternize during Scottish games at Jones's Wood. As the clans ceased to have a military function, the landowning chiefs began to demand rent from their tenants, which motivated many to emigrate.

native region too barren to support their population. The defeat of the clans at Culloden in 1746 set off a further chain of social and economic consequences in the Scottish Highlands. Before 1746, the wealth of estates had been counted in numbers of fighting men, not in currency. As the clans ceased to have a military function, the landowning chiefs sought to exact rent from their primary leaseholders, the *tacksmen*.

A tack (lease) had hitherto been held by an officer in exchange for his military service to the landowner. The tacksman's function was to organize subtenants as foot soldiers. This lieutenancy was a prestigious position to occupy, and the tacksmen did not want to relinquish it. Their role, however, had become obsolete. Rather than adjust to paying rent, many of the tacksmen migrated to North America. Angered that they were being shut out of a comfortable position, they incited their subtenants to emigrate with them. The tacksmen believed that they could establish themselves as chiefs in North America, and the subtenants agreed to go because they felt that their way of life was threatened. In 1773, Samuel Johnson noted:

> Whole neighborhoods formed parties for removal; so that departure from their native country is no longer exile. He that goes thus accompanied . . . sits down in a better climate, surrounded by his kindred and his friends: they carry their language, their opinions, their popular songs, and hereditary merriment: they change nothing but the place of their abode.

Despite the traditional Scottish lament that the people were driven from the land by the greed of the wealthy who brought poverty to the masses, during the 18th century emigration from Scotland and economic progress within Scotland were complementary phenomena. Migration increased dramatically at the same time as vast economic improvement for the majority of the country's people. For most, the decision to emigrate during this period was a conservative one. Although some Scots recognized the abundant opportunities available in the New World, most migrated in hopes of preserving their accustomed feudal social structure by transplanting it to a new place.

That the English government and the landlords opposed emigration and tried to prevent it confirms this theory. Failing to understand the reasons for emigration, government officials wrongly attributed it to contractors who arranged voyages to the New World. The English feared that Scots would adopt the ideas of liberty and equality that had emerged in the North American colonies. They neither wanted to lose Scots who could fight in the king's army nor wanted the rebellious colonists to gain them. In 1773, Parliament required that all ships carrying emigrants register their passengers before departing; many did not comply. In 1775, emigration from Scotland was prohibited altogether. Though migration came to a virtual standstill during the American Revolution, it resumed again in the early 1780s. Still opposing emigration in 1803, Parliament passed the Ship's Passenger Act, ostensibly to prevent abuses such as overcrowding but secretly designed to drive the prices of fares too high to be affordable for most emigrants.

Some colonies offered inducements to entice potential immigrants to move to North America. For instance, North Carolina offered to waive taxes, and several Middle Atlantic colonies offered land and easy naturalization. The greatest inducement, however, was permission to wear the tartan, unfettered by the clan-breaking legislation of the English.

Moving to North America

Beginning in the 1730s, emigration increased considerably, with the high point occurring in the late 1760s and early 1770s. An economic depression in Scotland in the 1770s swelled the flow with Lowlanders, who had typically been more prosperous than their northern neighbors. The actual numbers are incomplete and inexact. Estimates suggest that 20,000 left between 1763 and 1773 and 30,000 from 1773 to 1775. Between the years 1768 and 1775, there were 20,245 recorded Scottish immigrants in North America, though many were probably not counted. The total migration over the course of the 18th century was probably about 80,000. During this period, when the substantial majority of immigrants from other countries were single men of prime working age, approximately 70 percent of Scottish immigrants came in family groups. The age range of Scottish immigrants was also broad: 25 percent were children under 15 years old and 40 percent were over 25. Only the elderly were not largely represented.

Most of the 18th-century emigrants were not impoverished. Almost all paid their own fare for the voyage, either in cash or through indenture (an agreement under which an immigrant worked for a person for a specified period of time in return for the payment of passage). One indication of the relative wealth of the emigrants was that so many paid in cash. In fact, the loss of specie was one of the significant motivations for government opposition to emigration. Although very few of the emigrants were wealthy—as indeed very few Scots were—it is important to note that the 18th-century emigrants were not entirely lacking in resources the way their 19th-century successors were to be.

In addition to having some material resources, the immigrants were relatively well educated. The Reformation in Scotland had stressed education to ensure that

From his pulpit, religious reformer John Knox (1514–72) rails against Mary, Queen of Scots (in white). Largely responsible for the establishment of Presbyterianism in Scotland, Knox preached throughout the country against Catholicism and the Catholic monarch Mary. He wrote six tracts dealing with religious issues in Scotland, including The First Blast of the Trumpet Against the Monstrous Regiment of Women *(1558), in which he denounced rule by women.*

everyone could read the Bible and be attentive to their own salvation. John Knox, in his *First Book of Discipline*, set forth a plan for educating all the people of Scotland. It called for an elementary school in every parish, secondary schools in convenient locations accessible to all, and universities to educate future leaders in science, philosophy, and the ministry. Although Knox's plan was never fully realized, the educational system in Scotland was remarkably successful by the mid-18th century. Schools were open to everyone without regard for wealth, social standing, or religious affiliation. Much of the populace was literate, and many simple farmers read the classics such as Homer's *Iliad* in translation.

A great intellectual flowering known as the Scottish Enlightenment began in Scotland in the latter half of the 18th century. This period of intellectual progress that celebrated human reason was centered in the Scottish universities, which were both more numerous and more open-minded than those of England during the same years. For example, the historian Peter Hume Brown notes that the theories of Sir Isaac Newton were being taught at Edinburgh at the same time that they

This drawing depicts the College of Glasgow as it appeared in the 17th century. Scotland's universities were the seat of a great intellectual flowering in the 18th century known as the Scottish Enlightenment. Many graduates of Scottish universities immigrated to North America to pursue teaching careers, passing along the ideas of the Scottish Enlightenment to their American students.

were still being refuted at Oxford and Cambridge. The result of this educational reform and advance was an immigrant group far better educated than most others.

Although emigrants during this time were from both the Highlands and Lowlands, the majority were Highlanders. The most dramatic departures were from the islands: Skye, North and South Uist, Lewes, Arran, Jura, Gigha, and Islay. In an October 1773 entry to *The Journal of a Tour to the Hebrides with Samuel Johnson, L.L.D.*, Scottish writer James Boswell described a scene that vividly illustrates just how pervasive emigration had become:

> In the evening the company danced as usual.
> We performed, with much activity, a dance
> which, I suppose, the emigration from Sky[e]
> has occasioned. They call it *America*. A brisk reel
> is played. Each of the couples, after the common
> *involutions* and evolutions, successively whirls
> round in a circle, till all are in motion; and the
> dance seems intended to shew how emigration
> catches, till a whole neighborhood is set afloat.

Events of Passage

Conditions for those "set afloat" varied widely. Some emigrants suffered horribly on their transatlantic voyage, while others were relatively comfortable. Contractors operated for a profit and functioned quietly. Often ships departed from deserted Highland ports, attracting little attention. There are few records of the contractors' work except those that relate mishaps and disasters, which were frequent. Ships were usually overcrowded and often did not carry sufficient provisions, and outbreaks of epidemic disease such as measles and smallpox were common.

The first party of Highlanders to go to Pictou, a village in Nova Scotia, had a harrowing journey on the *Hector*. Its hull was so rotted that passengers could pick

An 1817 drawing shows the village of Pictou, Nova Scotia, one of the principal early settlements established by Scottish immigrants in Canada.

the wood apart with their fingers. A gale off the coast of Newfoundland delayed them by 14 days, and the provisions that were not ruined by mold were quickly exhausted. Dysentery (a disease characterized by severe diarrhea) and smallpox broke out, resulting in the death of 18 children. An even more tragic case was that of the *Nancy*, which embarked at Dornoch in Sutherland in September 1773, carrying 280 men, women, and children. Of the original number, 81 immigrants—including 50 children—died during the voyage, many the victims of starvation.

Although some captains clearly were quite negligent, others treated their passengers well. When the *Favourite* docked in New York in August 1773 after 9 weeks at sea, an observer wrote that the 140 passengers were "mostly young, and all remarkably healthy, well looking people, having had neither sickness nor death on the voyage, except a young child, who was ill before it came aboard." In September 1773, James Boswell described the *Nestor* in this way: "The accommodation for the emigrants was very good. . . . A long ward I may call it, with a row of beds on each side, every one of which was the same size every way, and fit to contain four people."

A New Home

Weary and anxious, the newly arrived immigrants were eager to find communities of others similar to themselves. During the 17th century, most Scottish immigrants settled in the southern and Middle Atlantic region. Immigrants of the 18th century also followed this pattern. The main sites of Highland settlement in the United States were the Cape Fear River valley in North Carolina, the Mohawk and Upper Hudson valleys in New York, and the Altamaha River valley in Georgia. In Canada, the main settlement was at Pictou in Nova Scotia and on Prince Edward Island.

The immigrants of the 18th century did not fit easily into North American society, and many did not particularly want to fit in. The first obstacle to their assimilation was language. The Lowlanders spoke broad Scots, a heavily accented English dialect that was difficult to understand. Most of the Highlanders spoke Gaelic, which separated them completely from their English-speaking neighbors. In Virginia, for instance, local courts had to retain Gaelic interpreters for the Jacobite exiles.

Because the Highlanders chose to hold themselves apart, the Cape Fear Valley remained distinctly Scottish for some time. Gaelic continued to be spoken there into the 20th century. In fact, Gaelic was so prevalent in the region that non-Scots came to speak it as well, which sometimes surprised newly arrived Scots. One story tells of a Highland woman who had just come to the colonies. She overheard two men speaking Gaelic and went to join them in conversation. When she entered the room, she discovered much to her surprise that the two men were black.

The Highlanders were also set apart by their distinctive dress. Trying to perpetuate the old ways, the transplanted Scots clung to their traditional mode of dress. In *Colonists from Scotland, 1707–1783*, Scottish historian Ian C. C. Graham notes several incidents illustrating this. For instance, when the governor of Georgia visited the Scottish colony at Darien in 1736, he found the settlers wearing kilts and carrying broadswords, shields, and muskets—all of which were forbidden in Scotland. The Native Americans whom Lachlan Campbell encountered after arriving in North America were so taken by his clothing that they asked him to settle among them. But when 350 Highlanders landed at Wilmington, North Carolina, the town officials there were so terrified by the Scots' warlike attire and foreign tongue that they considered forcing them all to swear an oath to behave peacefully. Highlanders were often jubilant at having the freedom to wear their feudal garb. When the *Hector* docked at Pictou, the passengers celebrated by donning kilts, dirks (long daggers), and claymores (swords), and the bagpipes were played as they disembarked.

Though their speech and dress set them apart, it was the political loyalties of the Scots that most greatly affected their assimilation into North American society. Unlike the Scotch-Irish (who fiercely resented the English for causing great disruption and bloodshed in Ulster), nearly all the Scots were loyal to the English king. The reasons for their loyalty are complex. Scotland had, after all, only recently been united with England, and prior to the union the countries had warred almost continuously. Ironically, it was their traditionalism that made the Scots Loyalists. The clan system instilled strict obedience to the chief, and the chiefs were loyal to the English king. Set upon retaining and perpetuating this social structure in the New World, they followed the tastes of their leaders, just as they had followed them to North America. Temperament was also a factor. The Scots were fundamentally conservative, and the revolutionary role was not one in which they felt comfortable.

The Lowland Scots adapted to North American society more easily and were assimilated more readily than their Highland compatriots. Although their speech was accented, it was not foreign, as was the Gaelic spoken by the Highlanders. Furthermore, they were not as attached to the idea of establishing a feudal social structure and thus did not feel compelled to live in Scottish settlements. Instead, they moved into existing towns and farming communities. Similarly, their politics were not as strictly conservative as the Highlanders. Dispersed as individuals, the Scottish allegiance and identity of many of the Lowlanders was less readily evident to outsiders.

The historical role of early U.S. frontiersmen has wrongly been attributed to the Scottish. In fact, it was the Scotch-Irish who settled the "backcountry" (western North Carolina and the central Appalachian Mountains), battled the Indians, and wrested farms out of the dense forests. The Scots, by contrast, made their homes along the seaboard, in areas that had been inhabited by Europeans for some time. Indeed, there was little contact between the Scots and the Scotch-Irish. Only in a few towns in western Pennsylvania and New England did they live together. The Scotch-Irish, who outnumbered the Scots by three to one, were a rougher,

McCausland's shipyard, dry dock, and sawmill, located in Rondout, New York, flourished in the late 19th century. Many Scottish immigrants became successful entrepreneurs and merchants.

more combative lot (largely because of the brutality they had experienced in Ireland), and their politics were exactly opposite those of the Loyalist Scots.

Many of the Scots became traders, clerks, and shopkeepers in the United States. The area they settled in North Carolina became a thriving, commercial crossroads between the rural backcountry, where crops and livestock were raised, and the tidewater ports, which brought in finished goods from Europe. The mercantilist Scots traded with Glasgow—which grew into a commercial giant—as well as Bristol, London, and the West Indies.

The Scots were aggressive and innovative merchants. In the Carolinas and Virginia, they bought lumber, cattle, and tobacco directly from the planters and established monopolies so they could control prices. They set up stores in the backcountry when they found that the towns were already controlled by British merchants. It seemed as if they had more energy than their competitors, as well as tremendous enthusiasm for material success. In Canada, the Scots entered the fur trade of the Northwest and eventually came to dominate it.

As the Scots seized every chance to advance themselves, they acquired—like most enterprising and identifiable ethnic minorities—a reputation for being acquisitive and clannish. In short, they were disliked for their success. Their entrepreneurial skills were not admired then as they are now; instead, they were seen as vulgar and somewhat menacing. Because the Scots acted as an interest group with great success and because they had formed clubs and aid societies, they became suspect among other Americans.

The Scots formed charitable societies to assist other Scots and to maintain social ties with them. There were several of these societies, the first being the Scots' Charitable Society of Boston, which was formed in the 1650s. Most, however, were known as St. Andrew's Societies and were started in the mid-18th century in cities such as Charleston (founded in 1729), Philadel-

(continued on page 57)

KEEPING THEIR
HERITAGE ALIVE

Overleaf: *Scottish Americans proudly display their clan tartans during a parade at the Grandfather Mountain Highland Games in North Carolina. Beginning in the colonial period, nearly 1.5 million Scots have immigrated to North America. In the United States today, more than 10 million people claim some Scottish heritage.*

The president of the New York Caledonian Club presents the haggis (on platter), a traditional Scottish dish, to the members of the club during its celebration of Robert Burns's birthday. These annual observances, organized by Scottish societies across North America, usually include the reading of the Scottish poet's works.

The Royal Scottish Country Dance Society enjoys a festive night of traditional dances. Scottish Americans have founded approximately 300 Scottish societies throughout the United States and Canada to foster pride in their ancestry.

Scottish Americans flock to the many Scottish games held throughout the United States. These outdoor festivals include events such as Highland dancing and traditional contests of strength and skill. Above: A competitor in the Grandfather Mountain Highland Games strains to throw a 28-pound weight. Top right: A group of teenagers compete in a dance contest at the Delco Scottish Games in Pennsylvania. Bottom right: At the Scottish Games in Alexandria, Virginia, a contestant balances a caber in preparation for his attempt in the caber toss competition. In earlier days, the caber was a small tree trunk, but telephone poles are now used in the game.

Professor Jim MacIntosh (right) of Carnegie-Mellon University teaches a student to play the bagpipe, a wind instrument popular in Scotland. The university, located in Pittsburgh, is the only school in the country that offers a bagpipe major.

*Band members, wearing the tartans of their respective clans,
perform at the Alexandria Scottish Games. Modern clan tartans,
woolen fabrics with plaid designs, have no relevance to the contemporary political or social realities of Scotland and are mostly
inaccurate reconstructions designed during the late 19th century.*

A young musician participates in the fiddling championships at the Alexandria Scottish Games. North Americans of Scottish descent remain proud of their cultural heritage, even if they are only part Scottish or if their families have lived in North America for many generations.

(continued from page 48)

phia (1749), Savannah (1750), and New York (1756). In addition, there were scattered social groups such as the Tuesday Club in Annapolis, which was begun by a Jacobite in 1745. Though some included in their charters the support of indigents of all nationalities, the emphasis was clearly Scottish and the members were almost always a select group of influential Scottish Americans.

The Scots not only were successful in business, but they also became increasingly powerful in the colonial government, compounding the suspicion and envy of other colonists. There were, for instance, Scottish officers in both Scottish and English regiments, which provoked English resentment. In the colonial government, the Scots exercised influence and power wholly out of proportion to their meager numbers. Between 1707 and 1783, there were 30 governors and lieutenant

The St. Andrew's Society of Montreal holds its annual ball in 1878. Scots often formed charitable societies to provide financial assistance to other Scottish immigrants and to maintain social ties with fellow Scots.

governors of Scottish origin. And the Scots often practiced favoritism, giving civil posts to other Scots solely because of their national heritage. The strong political and economic ties between Scotland and the Scots in the colonies were obvious and became a growing source of alarm and anger as the colonies moved toward revolution.

Indeed, some colonists even blamed the offending actions of the English Parliament on the influence of Scots at the British court. Reflecting on the growing tensions between England and the colonies, a Bostonian wrote to an Englishman in 1775:

> Your king seems infatuated with a parcel of Scotsmen and Jacobites. At least this is the best excuse that can be made for his conduct, and keeping them about him. If this was not the case, he would have removed his evil councillors long since, and thereby healed this unhappy quarrel.

Ezra Stiles, the president of Yale University (1778–95), wrote with great distaste about "the Scots' Perfidy & Tyranny and Enmity to America." His comments point to the perilous position that separatism and success had created for the Scots by the time of the Revolution:

> The Policy of Scotland & all the governmental Ideas of the Body of that People, are abhorrent to all Ideas of Liberty & are full of vigorous tyrannical Superiorities & Subordinations. . . . Let us boldly say, for History will say it, that the whole of this War is so far chargeable to the Scotch Councils, & to the Scotch as a Nation (for they have nationally come to it) as that had it not been for them, this Quarrel had never happened.

Ian C. C. Graham points out that in the pre–Civil War South there was an economic motivation for the dislike of the Scots. As the Scots became dominant in the Virginia tobacco trade, they extended credit to the wealthy planters. The planters were wasteful and soon found themselves in debt to the Scots. When Glasgow experienced a financial slump in the early 1770s, the Scottish-American merchants were forced to call in their debts and resort to the use of gold and silver. Credit was curtailed, and cash was tight. The planters, alarmed by their own debts, blamed the colony's economic troubles on the "foreign" element and on Scottish selfishness. Though these accusations were unjust, they played upon existing suspicions and could be disguised as patriotism.

The Revolutionary War

Not every Scot opposed the revolutionary war. For instance, John Witherspoon, a prominent clergyman and educator, played a critical role in the move for independence. Naval hero John Paul Jones and William Hyslop, an organizer of the Boston Tea Party, were also Scots. More intangibly, the Scottish Enlightenment provided some of the philosophical impetus for independence, and its political theories are evident in the U.S. Constitution and Bill of Rights.

Most members of the Scottish settlements in the South and in New York, however, took the side of the English. Though not all Scots were Loyalists, *Scot* and *Tory* became synonymous terms. Thousands of Scots either joined in arms with English soldiers or simply failed to support the patriots. The Scots who actually took up arms against the revolutionaries were defeated. The Battle of King's Mountain, North Carolina, for instance, was waged between Highlanders and patriots. After being defeated in a battle at Cross Creek, many local Scottish merchants were taken prisoner and their shops closed. The patriots took about 800 members of the North Carolina Scottish regiment prisoner. They deported the officers to Canada, where the majority stayed to settle in the Maritime Provinces.

A Scottish regiment musters itself prior to the Battle of King's Mountain. The American victory at King's Mountain proved crucial in the ultimate defeat of the English. During the revolutionary war, Scots loyal to England occasionally fought against Scotch-Irish patriots.

Scots in Norfolk swore an oath of allegiance to the English while the town was under their control. When Norfolk was taken by the patriots a month later, General Henry Lee ordered that the home of the wealthiest Scottish merchant be burned to discourage Scots from aiding the English. In December 1776, the Virginia House of Delegates and the governor, Patrick Henry, ordered that all "natives of Great Britain who were partners with agents, storekeepers, assistant storekeepers, or clerks for any merchants in Great Britain" leave the state within 40 days. Though some Scots remained in Richmond and Petersburg, there was a great exodus.

North Carolina, South Carolina, and Maryland all forced Scots to take an oath that they would fight against the English. Rather than do so, many Scots moved to Canada or returned to Scotland. The Mohawk Valley in New York was the third great arena of Scottish Loyalist activity. Most of the Loyalists were more recent immigrants and, as in the South, most were Highlanders.

They fought under Sir John Johnson and when ultimately defeated withdrew to Ontario, where they founded Glengarry County.

After the Revolution

After the war, the inordinate amount of influence enjoyed by the Scots in U.S. society vanished entirely. Only two men of Scottish origin signed the Declaration of Independence. The Scots' loss of political and economic power was entirely the consequence of their failure to support the colonies' break with England. During the last years of the 18th century, the focus of Scottish migration shifted from the Carolinas and New York to Canada. Though Scots continued to stream into North Carolina, they preferred to live in Canada under English rule. Loyalists fleeing the United States were early settlers of Ontario and New Brunswick, and subsequent immigrants also settled in Nova Scotia and on Prince Edward Island. A number of soldiers who fought during the Revolution in the Royal Highland Regiments settled in Canada after being discharged, and many received farmland for free.

The Scots in Canada lived comfortable lives and did not seem to have regretted their move. Patrick Campbell traveled to Canada in 1791 and noted the sentiments of his fellow migrants: "They blessed their stars that they had left Scotland, while they had something left to pay their way [and] regretted only [losing] the beautiful sight of the Highland hills." These sentiments were echoed in the 20th century by the renowned economist John Kenneth Galbraith after spending a damp and chilly day in the Highland home of his ancestors being filmed for a television program. When asked what he thought of the land his forebears left to go to Canada, he replied, "It is impossible to believe that my ancestors made a mistake!"

Flora Macdonald, who arrived in North Carolina in 1775, returned to Scotland four years later when her husband Allan Macdonald, a brigadier general in the English army, was captured and imprisoned by the Americans. The war prompted many Loyalist Scots to return to Scotland or move to Canada. Macdonald had earlier become a heroine in Scotland by helping Prince Charles Edward Stuart escape to France after the Battle of Culloden.

In 1924, a group of Scots join in singing "Flora Macdonald's Lament" as their passenger ship leaves Scotland for Canada. During the 19th and 20th centuries, thousands of Scots immigrated to North America in search of better economic opportunities.

THE NINETEENTH AND TWENTIETH CENTURIES: MASSIVE MIGRATION

After the American Revolution, migration grew in volume with each succeeding decade, slowed only by England's wars with France (1793–1815). Unlike the highly influential immigrants of the 18th century, the post–revolutionary war immigrants were mainly underprivileged and impoverished. The critical roles played by the tacksman and the private contractor in the migrations of the 18th century no longer existed in the subsequent waves of migration. Instead, Scots came out of necessity, pushed from Scotland by a variety of economic pressures. Rather than hindering emigration, the government would begin to promote it as the 19th century progressed. The causes of the large-scale emigration of the 19th and 20th centuries differed, depending on the region that the emigrant left.

The Highlands: Enclosure and Clearance

In the 19th century, the Highlands experienced the full brunt of the modernizing process that had begun during the agricultural revolution in the previous century. Although abandoning feudal practices was ultimately beneficial for Scotland, it seemed that every improvement first caused hardships for the poor.

The most significant changes were those in land tenure. Many tenant farmers were poor and used antiquated farming methods. Landlords, interested in improving the output of their holdings, raised rents and sought to introduce more productive farming methods. To implement agricultural improvements, however, they first had to eliminate the old "run-rig" lots, open land held by joint tenure with loosely defined strips or ridges of land for each tenant. The trend of "enclosing" jointly held lands into fenced fields had begun in the late 18th century and now swept the countryside. Early enclosure measures limited the Highlanders' access to free grazing, making it even more difficult to make ends meet.

Having tried to prevent emigration throughout the previous century, the landlords now abruptly realized that their land was divided among far too many to be efficient or economical. A government brief written in 1819 coldly notes the landlords discovering that

> the consequences of throwing obstacles in the way
> of emigration are now come to an alarming height
> . . . their Estates are consumed by the useless
> pernicious & increasing population; they are now
> eager to get rid of the people as they were formerly
> to retain them; but it is too late, the people have
> consumed the means they formerly possessed
> & are become so poor they cannot transport them-
> selves to any other place.

Increasingly, landlords sought to turn their property into large sheep or cattle farms. Land that had been

Scottish Evictions, *an 1815 painting by Sir David Wilkie, depicts rent collectors evicting a family. During the clearances of the 18th and 19th centuries, Highland landlords expelled tenants from their ancestral homes to make way for larger tracts of grazing land. The clearances caused much hardship for the masses and much bitterness among Highlanders.*

home to the same clan for centuries suddenly was to be turned into empty pasture. Even though their small farms were poor, Highlanders did not want to leave their ancestral glens, and thousands of reluctant Highlanders had to be forcibly removed from the land. These evictions were called "clearances," and they caused great and lasting bitterness among the Highlanders.

In some cases, landlords attempted to handle the surplus population by paying tenants' fares to North America. Other clansmen were relocated closer to the coast onto small, individually held plots of land called "crofts." There, it was thought, they could continue subsistence farming and supplement their crops with fishing, weaving, and gathering kelp (kelp was used for alkaline, which was needed in the manufacture of glass and soap). Unfortunately, crofters were often displaced again as the clearances took in more and more ground. With the advent of automated looms and better sources of alkaline, the crofters' supplemental means of income collapsed, and they were left on parcels of land too small to support their families.

The Highlanders, who had lived on the same land and loyally served its owners for generations, perceived the clearances as a profound betrayal. Although the agricultural improvements that the nobles implemented ultimately benefited Scotland, the displaced and threatened Highlanders perceived only the harm done. They felt that the chiefs suddenly loved sheep better than men. Misunderstanding on both sides eventually led to violence. One of the lowest points of the clearances occurred at Glengarry in 1853, when entire families were forced onto ships and those who hid in the forests were hunted down like animals.

Sad as the story of the clearances is, it should be noted that other factors were at work. Advances in medicine had brought about a marked increase in population. Over the course of the century, the population of Scotland increased by 75 percent to 4.5 million in 1899. The larger population both increased competition for land and made improved methods of crop production necessary. Overpopulation became a fundamental problem that could only be solved by emigration.

The Lowlands: Unemployment and Unhappiness

For those who did not leave Scotland during the clearances, few alternative occupations existed in the Highlands, and many had to move to towns or cities to find work. Many sought jobs in the textile industries of the Lowlands.

The cotton industry, centered in Ayr, experienced a tremendous expansion. Between 1780 and 1822, the annual output tripled to 36 million yards, and the number of handloom weavers multiplied in response to this growth. Although spinning had been quickly automated with the advent of steam power, weaving remained a manual task, partly because of the vast pool of cheap labor supplied by displaced Highlanders. This situation changed in the 1830s as automation finally took over the weaving process. Even the master weavers began to face declining income and eventual unemployment. The linen industry, centered in Paisley and Glasgow, had likewise grown during the 18th century. It went through a similar transformation, and by the middle of the 19th century, linen weavers had largely been replaced by machines.

Throughout the Lowlands, industry thrived as Scotland embraced the advances of the Industrial Revolution. Huge linen factories sprang up in Dundee, Lanark (near Glasgow), and Renfrew. The increase in sheep farming spurred the woolen industry, especially in the Border region, where tweed was made. Heavy industry burgeoned with the discovery of coal and iron ore deposits and the perfection of blast-furnace smelting. The shipbuilding industry grew, new mines were opened, roads were improved, and canals were built. Urban population mushroomed. Glasgow, for instance, grew from 12,500 in 1708 to 200,000 in 1831. Whereas approximately 500,000 men were farmers in 1801, only 200,000 farmed at the end of the century, reflecting both the shift to other occupations and the success of agricultural improvements.

Industrial advances and the growth of cities brought Scotland into the modern world, but they also brought hardship. The gap between the rich and the poor grew

Textile workers supervise the looms in a weaving mill in New Lanark in 1843. The textile industry boom of the late 17th and early 18th centuries provided employment for many Lowlanders and displaced Highlanders, but the advent of automated looms in the 1830s hurled many Scots back into the ranks of the unemployed.

Residents of a Glasgow slum gather in a dank alley. As the gap between Scotland's rich and poor increased during the 19th century, many Scots looked to emigration as the only way to improve their economic and social situation.

ever wider during the 19th century. The landed aristocracy, which still held sway, was joined by a new class of wealthy merchants. At the other end of society, however, there was terrible poverty. Crowded and miserable slums multiplied in Edinburgh and Glasgow. Housing was scarce, and wages often inadequate to pay even the lowest rents. Work in the factories, furnaces, and shipyards was exhausting and often dehumanizing. The unskilled labor market was permanently and vastly oversupplied by migrants from the Highlands and from Ireland, resulting in very low wages and chronic unemployment. In the Lowlands, industrial society left a large number of people behind, and many others detested its demands.

For the Lowlander, as for the Highlander, emigration offered the possibility of a better life. Many of the emigrants from the Lowlands were artisans who faced technological unemployment. They were skilled and literate individuals. The historian Charlotte Erikson has written about the complex motivations for leaving cited in the letters of emigrants. She has noted that those who left in the 1820s, 1830s, and 1840s did so out of utter economic necessity. Those who left after 1850, however, did so more out of the fear that they would become unemployed than from actual unemployment.

Many perceived emigration as an investment and used all of their resources to pay for the voyage to North America. (Some were aided by remittances from North America.) In fact, one of the reasons given for leaving was that incomes in Scotland did not allow people to save money. Among those who had worked in factories, there was a great desire to be self-employed. Erikson cited a powerful strain of agrarian utopianism, finding many who thought farming would allow them leisure and freedom. They were eager to be rid of

Pioneers begin the work to build Savannah, Georgia, in the 1730s. Similar to many other European immigrants, Scots were drawn to the idealized portrayal of North America as the land of opportunity, believing that owning their own farms would provide them with independence, wealth, and leisure.

Andrew Carnegie (1835–1919) moved from Dunfermline, Scotland, to Allegheny, Pennsylvania, with his family in 1848. He became the archetypal self-made man, rising from factory worker to baron of the U.S. iron and steel industry. In his book The Gospel of Wealth *(1900), Carnegie wrote that "the man who dies rich dies disgraced," and he donated much of his fortune to support a wide range of philanthropic projects, ranging from public parks and libraries to research and educational foundations.*

government regulation, high taxes, and the economic uncertainties of the modern marketplace. For these Scots, the land and liberty of the North American frontier seemed like paradise.

Another major impetus was the fear of losing one's status in society. Thus, healthy pride made many willing to endure the hardships of moving to another country. A clergyman, for instance, wrote to his son who had moved to Indiana:

> Had you [stayed] here you would have lived somehow, but you could not have continued in the society you have been used to. Here the smaller stations of property appear [to be] gradually wearing into pauperism and the prospect before us is unpromising indeed.

For both the Highlander and the Lowlander, letters, news, and even songs from Canada and the United States offered a source of hope. The great industrialist Andrew Carnegie was born in Dunfermline in 1835, the son of a handloom weaver. As a child, he would hear his parents sing:

> To the West, to the West, to the land of the free,
> Where the mighty Missouri rolls down to the sea;
> Where a man is a man if he's willing to toil,
> And the humblest may gather the fruits of the soil;
> Where children are blessings, and he who hath most
> Has aid for his fortune and riches to boast.
> Where the young may exult and the aged may rest,
> Away, far away, to the land of the West.

It was this optimistic ballad and the hopeful letters from relatives already in the United States that led his family to emigrate in 1848. Only 13 years old at the time, Carnegie, like many other immigrant children of the era, went to work immediately in a factory. By the age of 16, he too was writing letters to family and friends in Scotland, touting the opportunities available in his adopted land.

Immigration Statistics in the Nineteenth Century

The figures for migration in the first years of the 19th century are imprecise. One source notes that 10,000 went to Canada in 1801–2, and another reports only 6,000 did. In 1803, it was either 10,000 or 20,000, though both agree it was 15,000 in 1804. The United States began keeping official immigration records in 1819. They indicate that in the first half of the 19th century, most Scots went to Canada. Between 1820 and 1851, only 10,525 Scots came to the United States. This began to change after mid-century, and from 1852 onward several thousand Scots immigrated to the United States virtually every year, peaking during the 1850s and the 1880s. After 1870, the numbers of Scottish immigrants entering the United States exceeded 10,000 a year, slightly more than half of the total number of emigrants leaving Scotland. In all, 478,224 Scots immigrated to the United States between 1852 and 1910.

At the close of the 19th century, the Scottish Highlands were so depopulated that there were few left to migrate. Many of the western isles had experienced a population loss of 75 percent. Testifying silently to the great exodus were hundreds of empty, ruined houses scattered across the sheep pastures.

The Nineteenth-Century Immigrants

What was it like for an individual to pack up and leave his family and friends to go off to an unknown and distant country? One such individual was Robert Brownlee, who was born in 1813 in Bonkle, a small Lowland town. Brownlee was one of eight children, and his father was a laborer and his mother tamboured (embroidered) to help make ends meet. Trained as a stonemason, Brownlee decided in the middle of work one day to go to the United States. It was 1836, and he figured that New York, which was rebuilding after the great fires of 1835, would need masons. Brownlee went to Glasgow and booked passage on a ship that was to leave several days later. His family was saddened by his impending departure, but Brownlee himself showed remarkable nonchalance:

> Mother began to realize how things stood, only two days to make shirts out of home made lint called harn shirts, strong enough to last till you got tired of them, which was not very long after I landed. . . . While these preparations were going on I was visiting my friends and relations, and besides I want you to know, I had sweethearts to be attended to.

Brownlee sailed on the *Tasso* with 21 other passengers, reaching New York after 6 weeks and 3 days at sea. Conditions were considerably better than they had been in the previous century; Brownlee suffered nothing worse than seasickness.

Areas of Settlement

The majority of Scottish emigrants in the early 19th century went to Canada, settling in the Maritime provinces and upper Canada. After mid-century, however, more and more Scots came to the United States. Once in the United States, immigrants often settled for a time in the port city where they had landed, usually Boston, New York, or Philadelphia. The rail system was completed in mid-century, allowing immigrants to settle throughout the country and press into the western frontier. By 1850, there were 5,000 Scots in Illinois, among them the founders of Chicago. Scots also settled in Missouri, and in Iowa their numbers increased from 700 to 3,000 from 1850 to 1860. Settlement in the Far West preceded that in the Midwest. In fact, Scots were some of the earliest non-Hispanic residents of California.

Adapting to Their New Land

The poor crofters who left Scotland in the 19th century had many more unhappy memories of their homeland than did their 18th-century predecessors. Their negative feelings for Scotland made the immigrants more willing and eager to become assimilated in North American society. The United States and Canada had changed as well, and now Scots were one group among many in a heterogeneous and rapidly growing population. Exceptions to this general rule did occur. For instance, Gaelic-speaking enclaves in Newfoundland and Cape Breton, founded in the 19th century, persisted well into the 20th century. In urban areas, however, the Protestant, English-speaking Scots blended in easily.

Occupations

Some Scottish immigrants hastened to the frontier to fulfill their dreams of owning their own farms. Others, like the Carnegies, took factory jobs in cities where their relatives were already settled. Those who arrived as families tended to seek farms, and many such families took the grueling overland trails west prior to the completion of the transcontinental railroad in 1867. Single men tended to take city jobs, laboring in construction or factory jobs to accumulate cash. Seeking economic advancement, many of these young men went to California in the gold rush of 1849.

Robert Brownlee was typical in that he settled for a time in his port of entry, New York. He was amazed by how much money he could make in a day as a stonecutter: two to three dollars, which seemed like a fortune to him. He commented:

> This is not all. We had coffee and beef-steak for breakfast, roast beef and pie for dinner, with fish every Friday. What a difference from boiled potatoes and salt. I enjoyed the change immensely.

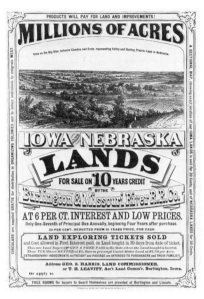

An 1873 advertisement beckons prospective homesteaders to the Iowa and Nebraska frontier. Many Scottish immigrants joined the rush of pioneers who moved into the unsettled western territories of the United States and Canada during the 19th century.

He saved $100 to send to his mother and then left the city for greater adventures. He went first to Raleigh, North Carolina, where stonemasons were needed for building the new city hall. From there he moved to Little Rock, Arkansas, where he fell in love. Like many other Scottish immigrants, Brownlee made his way by hard work, thriftiness, and a willingness to adapt. At various times, he worked as a mason, a bricklayer, a stonecutter, and a miner before setting off in 1849 for California.

There Brownlee found enough gold to start a supply business and eventually made enough money to return to Scotland (in 1852) for a visit and then to Arkansas to marry. With his bride, he returned to California, only to find that his partner had lost their money and could only offer a farm as compensation. With no knowledge of farming, Brownlee took over a Napa Valley farm and made it profitable. He and his wife lived there for 40 years, raising 6 children.

Families who went to the frontier with an idealistic vision of agrarian life were often disappointed. They found the task of carving a farm out of the wilderness to be desperately hard work. Their knowledge of farming was often imperfect, and the work to be done in bringing land under cultivation for the first time was prodigious. They suffered from a lack of goods and, more important, from a lack of markets. Transportation was primitive, and many services, such as schools, were scarce. They faced cholera, typhoid, malaria, and the loneliness of life on isolated farms.

Idealism about farming gave way to economic pragmatism. Ironically, those who had less money when they arrived tended to fare better because they did not feel that their standard of living had been drastically reduced. A few despaired and returned to Scotland. Others gave up their farms but remained in the West, populating the new towns and providing much-needed services. Many, however, poured all they had into their first farms and achieved, if not the paradise they had foreseen, a comfortable life.

A similar story is told by John Kenneth Galbraith (born October 15, 1908), an eminent economist and a former U.S. ambassador. His ancestors came to the Canadian wilderness in the 1830s, forced out of Scotland by the clearances. He writes fondly about the "good fortune" of the home his Scottish ancestors found:

The Pittendrugh family on their farm near Rapid City, Manitoba. Many Scottish immigrants like the Pittendrughs found life on frontier farms much different from their idealized vision.

Certainly it was a wonderful reward that it accorded those who came to it. To contend with the forests there unquestionably required a generation or two of demanding toil. (My great-grand-father seems to have succumbed at an early age to a falling tree.) Thereafter there were the broad fields of deep soil, free of stones and even

In 1927, a group of Scottish emigrants prepare for their journey to North America. Scottish immigration to North America increased following World War I, but after the 1920s, Scots no longer arrived in substantial numbers.

more intractable ledges, and soon there were pleasant and, certainly by all modern standards, spacious houses. And schools and churches and astonishing freedom from social conflict or tension. . . . In two or three generations not many of the Scotch in Elgin County would have exchanged places—or living standards—with those landed families who, in the Clearances, had forced their movement to the New World. Much has rightly been made of the courage and vigor of those who made and survived the initial journey into the wilderness. Less is made of the good fortune they or their children enjoyed after a few decades—or of the even greater talent for privation and suffering that was required of those who stayed behind.

The Twentieth Century

In sheer numbers, the greatest migration to the United States and Canada occurred in the 1920s. Ten years of economic blight after World War I sent more than 300,000 Scots to the United States. Most of these were unemployed Lowlanders. The 1920 census shows the majority of persons of Scottish birth were living in the northeastern and mid-Atlantic states, followed by Illinois, California, Ohio, and Michigan. Most (196,000) lived in cities, whereas only 58,000 lived in rural areas. Immigration between the world wars did little to alter the areas of settlement, but the number living on farms decreased to 49,000, and the number living in cities jumped to 230,000. The 1970 census figures showed that New York and California were home to the greatest number of people of Scottish descent.

The Sprunt family relaxes on the front porch of their home in Wilmington, North Carolina. James Sprunt (left) was a senior partner in Alexander Sprunt & Son, Inc., a large cotton-exporting company founded in 1878 by his Scottish father. Scottish immigrants, such as Alexander Sprunt, and their descendants have greatly contributed to the intellectual, spiritual, and economic growth of North America.

THE SCOTTISH CONTRIBUTION

Throughout the centuries, Scottish immigrants have had a meaningful effect on North American society and culture. Although the character of the contributions made by Scottish Americans has changed with each new wave of immigration, they have been notably influential in the fields of politics and law, the military, education and religion, medicine, science and industry, and the arts.

Politics and Law

From the very beginning of the United States, Scots have made valuable contributions to its government. Although the vast majority of Scots remained loyal to England during the Revolution, it should be noted that a few became leaders within the movement for independence. Two Scots—John Witherspoon of New Jersey and James Wilson of Pennsylvania—signed the Declaration of Independence, and Patrick Henry,

Alexander Hamilton (1755–1804) was the most influential Scottish American in U.S. history. Among his many accomplishments, he served valiantly in the revolutionary war and was the chief author of The Federalist *essays. As the first U.S. secretary of the Treasury, Hamilton developed an impressive and effective financial plan that created immediate faith in the government of the new nation.*

whose father was Scottish, vigorously supported the war effort as governor of Virginia (1776–79).

Perhaps the most influential Scottish-American statesman was Alexander Hamilton, who was born in Nevis (an English island colony in the West Indies) in 1755. Hamilton, whose father was a Scot, was sent to New York alone at a young age and enrolled at King's College (later renamed Columbia University) when he was 16 years old. Hamilton's education, however, was interrupted by the impending revolution. He was a patriot, and with characteristic dash and a thirst for distinction he joined the fray. He spoke at mass meetings, wrote for the *New York Journal*, and championed the colonists' cause in a number of pamphlets. People marveled that a teenager had such impressive argumentative skills and such a firm grasp of the issues; in fact, his anonymous writings were frequently attributed to older politicians, such as John Jay.

Early in 1776, Hamilton was granted the command of an artillery company. In the summer and fall campaigns, he fought with George Washington on Long Island, helped to fortify Harlem Heights, commanded two guns at White Plains, and that winter he participated in attacks on Trenton and Princeton. Washington recognized Hamilton's extraordinary intelligence and in March 1777 plucked him from the fighting ranks to serve as his personal secretary and aide-de-camp. As he became a trusted adviser to the general, Hamilton's correspondence with the Continental Congress and the states gave him an unparalleled opportunity to learn about the nation and its army.

The extraordinary creativity and incisiveness of Hamilton's political thought began to unfold in the correspondence that he maintained from 1771 to 1781 with various leaders of the emerging nation. In these letters, he carefully explained the defects of the Articles of Confederation (the precursor to the Constitution), set forth a detailed plan for revising the government, and proposed a Constitutional Convention.

A tendency toward irascibility and stubbornness tarnished Hamilton's passionate and decisive personality. A petty quarrel with Washington in 1782 prompted Hamilton to leave the general's service and return to the battlefield. Commanding an infantry regiment, he performed brilliantly at the siege of Yorktown, the scene of the English surrender.

After the war, Hamilton passed the bar. He took a seat in the Continental Congress in 1782 but resigned in 1783 after becoming annoyed with the feebleness of that body. He began a private law practice on Wall Street and threw himself into the battle for a stronger national government. In 1786, amid growing confusion over the powers of the government, a general commercial convention was held to discuss ways of facilitating interstate trade. Hamilton, eager for the chance to act, secured appointment as one of the two New York delegates. Although the convention itself failed, Hamilton managed to win a resolution recommending that a Constitutional Convention be held the following summer. It was a deft political maneuver and drove home the message that commercial cooperation between the states was impossible without strong political unity.

Hamilton played only a minor role at the Constitutional Convention. His greatest contribution, instead, was in securing the adoption of the Constitution. In July 1787, he began writing a series of distinctly ardent newspaper articles supporting ratification. These essays were collected and published in 1788 as *The Federalist*. Hamilton wrote 51 of the 85 essays himself and 3 more with James Madison. A brilliant work of political theory, *The Federalist* is part of the invaluable heritage of the Constitution, and its message was instrumental in securing the adoption of the document. At New York's convention to deliberate the ratification of the Constitution, Hamilton, with the help of John Jay and Robert Livingston, mounted a spectacular floor fight. They overthrew every objection against ratification, and by the sheer force of his brilliant and impassioned speeches, Hamilton changed the minds of the anti-Federalist majority.

In 1789, Washington selected Hamilton as the United States's first secretary of the Treasury. Although he had no practical experience in this field, Hamilton learned with characteristic speed. The nation faced a huge debt, but Hamilton's tremendous determination and tireless political efforts ensured that the government neither repudiated its many foreign loans nor failed to assume the states' debts. His proposals for levying import duties, creating an excise tax on alcohol, establishing a national bank and mint, and funding the assumption of the states' debts met with fierce opposition, but all were adopted. Hamilton's many briefs and reports established a national fiscal system, strengthened the central government, developed the resources of the young nation, and stimulated manufacturing. He created out of nothing a sound public credit and gave the country a viable circulating currency. For these achievements alone, he must rank as one of the most courageous and visionary of the United States's founders.

Hamilton's innate aggressiveness and tendency to meddle led him into conflict with other leaders of the young nation, particularly with Secretary of State Thomas Jefferson. Theirs was both a personal and a philosophical dislike, and Hamilton left the cabinet in 1795. Although his law practice was extraordinarily successful, Hamilton's lack of discretion and restraint made his transition out of public life bumpy at best. He disagreed with and resented President John Adams, at one point publishing a written attack upon the president that was perhaps his worst blunder. Yet he rose from this embarrassment during the 1800 election. Believing Aaron Burr to be unfit for the presidency, Hamilton supported Jefferson, despite their intense personal rivalry, and Jefferson was elected by the House of Representatives after the national election resulted in a deadlock. When Hamilton opposed Burr during Burr's campaign for the governorship of New York in 1804, he was once again able to thwart Burr's aspirations. Enraged, Burr challenged Hamilton to a duel.

On the morning of July 11, 1804, Aaron Burr—48 years old and the vice-president of the United States—and Alexander Hamilton, 49, faced each other in Weehawken, New Jersey, on the banks of the Hudson River. Burr had challenged Hamilton to a duel with pistols. Eerily, they stood on the same field where

As their seconds look on, Alexander Hamilton (left) and Vice-president Aaron Burr confront each other in Weehawken, New Jersey, on July 11, 1804. Burr challenged Hamilton to a duel of honor following Hamilton's incessant public insults and shrewd political maneuvers that had foiled Burr's political ambitions. After his adversary fired harmlessly over his head, Burr mortally wounded Hamilton.

Hamilton's eldest son, Philip, had been killed in a duel three years earlier. Each man held one of the pistols that had been used in that fatal contest. Hamilton had chosen the weapons; both guns had concealed hair triggers, enabling them to be fired by the slightest pressure. It is not known whether Hamilton was aware of the sensitive triggers, but his pistol shot harmlessly, its ball lodging high in a tree behind Burr. Burr aimed carefully, and his shot struck Hamilton in the liver. Hamilton fell and, according to witnesses at the scene, gasped that he never intended to fire. He died, in great pain, within 36 hours. The coroner's report described his death as willful murder, and Burr was indicted for homicide, although he was never tried on the charge.

A man of strong and logical intellect, Hamilton was the foremost orator of his era. A hard and efficient

pragmatist who believed in national wealth, strength, and order—but not particularly in individual liberty— his faith rested with the elite, not with the masses. Hamilton's realism was truly invaluable to the emergent nation, and though his elitism became outmoded, he had an incalculably great effect on the Republic.

Many descendants of Scottish immigrants have served in the judiciary, Congress, and in state and local governments. On the bench of the first Supreme Court, which heard its first case in 1789, sat two Scottish Americans—John Blair and James Wilson (Wilson also was a signer of the Declaration of Independence). Two other jurists of Scottish descent, John Rutledge and John Marshall, served as the second and the third chief justice (respectively) of the Supreme Court. During his 35-year tenure, Marshall wrote many pivotal decisions that strengthened the powers of the federal government. Adlai Stevenson served in the House of Representatives and as vice-president under Grover Cleveland from 1983 to 1897. His grandson, Adlai Stevenson II served one term as governor of Illinois and twice ran unsuccessfully for the presidency, losing to Dwight D. Eisenhower in 1952 and 1956. Presidents James Monroe, Ulysses S. Grant, Rutherford B. Hayes, and Theodore Roosevelt had some Scottish ancestry.

Woodrow Wilson, the 28th president of the United States, was born in Staunton, Virginia, in 1856. His father was a Presbyterian minister and a professor of theology; his mother, the daughter of a Scottish minister. As an undergraduate at the College of New Jersey (Princeton), Wilson excelled in debating and studied history and politics. Fascinated with the idea of a career in public service, he enrolled in the law school at the University of Virginia. Wilson abandoned law school in 1880 and started a legal practice in Atlanta. Disenchanted with the practice of law, he entered Johns Hopkins University in 1883 to study history. In 1885, Wilson's influential book *Congressional Government* was

John Marshall served as the chief justice of the U.S. Supreme Court from 1801 to 1835. Under his leadership, the Court strengthened the powers of the federal government by ruling that the government could legitimately exercise authority over all matters except those prohibited by the Constitution.

published, and as his dissertation it earned him his doctorate one year later.

Prior to his appointment as professor of jurisprudence and political economy at Princeton, Wilson taught at Bryn Mawr College and Wesleyan University. Though uninterested in specialized research, his intellectual rigor and philosophical liberalism earned him respect and attention. Wilson was a popular professor and traveling lecturer, and in June 1902, he was unanimously elected president of Princeton University.

Wilson's tenure as president was closely identified with educational reform. He was dissatisfied with the structure of undergraduate education at Princeton and believed that the lecture system did not encourage students to think for themselves. Wilson also felt that far too much emphasis was placed on athletics and social life. His remedy was an academic reform plan, the "preceptorial" system, and a program for residential and social life, the "quad" plan. The preceptorial system proposed small discussion groups to supplement lectures, and the quad plan sought to integrate students' social and intellectual lives by dividing the university into residential colleges on the British model. An integral part of Princeton's social snobbery was its upperclassmen's eating clubs, which were supported by wealthy East Coast alumni. The existence of these exclusive clubs, which were similar to fraternities on other campuses, offended Wilson's egalitarian principles and stood in the way of his plans for reform. Ultimately, he was not able to dislodge the private clubs and their elitist practices, but the preceptorial system was adopted and persists today.

Ironically, the lost battle over the eating clubs brought Wilson into the public eye and won him enormous favor as a champion of democratic ideals. In 1910, he was chosen as the Democratic candidate for the governorship of New Jersey. Stipulating that he be bound by no obligations of patronage, Wilson resigned from the university and was handily elected on November 8.

Woodrow Wilson (1856–1924), a descendent of Scottish and Scotch-Irish immigrants, enjoys an afternoon with his family. Before his appointment as president of Princeton University, Wilson was a professor at Bryn Mawr, Wesleyan University, and Princeton. After a successful term as governor of New Jersey, Wilson was elected president of the United States in 1912 and reelected in 1916.

The political bosses thought Governor Wilson would be naive and easily manipulated. They were shocked to find that the new governor was a powerful speaker and commanded enormous popular support. He successfully defied the Democratic party machine and pushed through a number of measures that curtailed corruption in government.

Wilson quickly caught the attention of national party leaders and with their support was nominated Democratic candidate for president. With the Republican party split between Roosevelt and former president William Taft, Woodrow Wilson easily won the 1912 presidential election. A conservative reformist, his agenda was dubbed the New Freedom. Again he fought for the interests of the common citizen against the powers of finance, industry, and commerce. His notable reform legislation included the Underwood tariff, which lowered protectionist barriers; the Federal Reserve Act, a currency reform program; the Federal Trade Commission Act; and the Clayton Anti-Trust Act, which broke up the nation's powerful industrial monopolies while permitting the growth of trade unions.

Wilson, a staunch pacifist, was reelected in 1916 on a platform of keeping the United States out of the war in Europe. He had been successful up to that time in maintaining U.S. neutrality while standing firm against German submarine attacks, which disrupted the right of U.S. citizens to travel freely and safely on international waters. But despite Wilson's concerted efforts to negotiate peace, the U.S. Congress declared war on Germany in March 1917.

Although Wilson had been determined to avoid U.S. involvement in the war, once the nation entered the war his leadership was distinguished. He instilled the American people with the willingness to make sacrifices and work together in a mutual endeavor to win the war. He had the judgment to appoint capable individuals to manage the war effort and the wisdom to let them carry out their work without political interference. Wilson supported military leaders, enabling them to build and supply a powerful armed force in France that finally numbered 2 million.

Most important, Wilson conveyed to Americans and to their allies the belief that they were fighting for peace. He maintained that the only basis for a lasting peace rested with a system of international cooperation that would ensure that no nation would be subject to aggression and that the seas would be free to all: "a virtual guarantee of territorial integrity and political independence" for all nations. These objectives and Wilson's war aims in general were embodied in his Fourteen Points, a plan that he presented to Congress in 1918. It was a momentous step for the United States, taking the nation, for the first time, squarely into both the arena of general questions of world peace and specific international territorial disputes.

The Germans, foreseeing their own defeat, seized upon Wilson's generous plan, making it their basis for the negotiation of peace. Wilson's plan offered Germany protection from the total defeat the European allies sought to exact. Wilson was anxious to encourage Ger-

man surrender in order to limit the losses of prolonged warfare. Though the Allies were bitter over their already enormous losses and irritated by the United States's usurpation of the peace initiative, Wilson's peace-seeking diplomacy actually resulted in complete victory for the Allies and prevented the bloody last ditch efforts into which the Germans would have been forced. On November 11, 1918, the armistice was signed.

Unfortunately, Wilson's general principles were difficult to translate into the specifics of a peace settlement that would please all of the nations involved. At the Paris Peace Conference, Wilson refused to accept that compromise was necessary. Although many of his noble principles were modified during the negotiations, Wilson was able to compel the inclusion of the League of

In March 1919, Woodrow Wilson (back row, center) poses with other members of the International Commission on the League of Nations. Wilson's tremendous sense of responsibility, keen intelligence, forceful oratorical skills, and sincere idealism made him both an effective president and an innovative world leader. He was a great visionary whose ideas provided the foundation for the creation of the United Nations.

General Douglas MacArthur (1880–1964) takes a break during a World War II strategy session. Serving with distinction in both world wars and the Korean War, MacArthur was one of the United States's most accomplished and controversial military leaders.

Nations Covenant in the peace treaty. All of the nations present at the negotiations signed the treaty except the United States. Without the reassurance of even its minor concessions, the U.S. Senate rejected the treaty, and, ironically, the nation that had originated the League of Nations never participated in the organization.

The Military

Scottish Americans have served with distinction in the military throughout the history of the United States. In the American Revolution, only a few Scots fought with the patriots, but several were dynamic leaders. General John Stark fought at Bunker Hill and participated in Washington's New Jersey campaign in the winter of 1776–77. General George Rogers Clark led his small band on successful expeditions into the Illinois territory, capturing several English strongholds. Another Scot, General Henry Knox, became the nation's first secretary of war in 1785.

General Winfield Scott, the grandson of a Scot who fought at the Battle of Culloden, served during the War of 1812 and later became the commanding general of the U.S. Army and led the nation's military efforts during the Mexican War (1846–48). During the Civil War, soldiers of Scottish ancestry served in both armies. Union generals of Scottish descent included John C. Breckenridge and Ambrose Burnside, and the Confederate army boasted such generals as Joseph Johnston, John Brown Gordon, and John B. Magruder.

Douglas MacArthur, the son of Civil War hero Lieutenant General Arthur MacArthur, was decorated for his service in World War I. He was the superintendent of the U.S. Military Academy at West Point (1919–22) and was promoted to full general upon becoming army chief of staff in 1930. MacArthur retired from the U.S. Army in 1937 to become field marshal of the Philippine army but returned to active duty when the United States entered World War II. He led a valiant but unsuccessful defense of the Philippines against a massive Japanese assault. In March 1942, he was ordered to Australia to become supreme Allied commander in the Southwest Pacific theater. In April 1945, MacArthur was named commander of all U.S. Army forces in the Pacific, and he accepted the surrender of Japan aboard the USS *Missouri* in Tokyo Bay on September 2, 1945. During the Korean War, MacArthur served as commander of the United Nations' defending forces. When China entered the conflict in support of North Korea, he publicly criticized President Harry S. Truman and advocated the bombing of Chinese bases in Manchuria and the backing of an invasion of China. These actions led Truman to relieve MacArthur of his command on April 11, 1951, on the grounds of insubordination. Although some viewed MacArthur as autocratic, he was one of the most successful military leaders in U.S. history.

Education and Religion

Scottish Americans have contributed greatly to the educational system in the United States. Most headmasters of primary and secondary schools in the colonies south of New York were Scottish, and they trained many leaders of the American Revolution. For example, the tutors of Thomas Jefferson and John Rutledge were Scottish immigrants.

Many academies, colleges, and universities were founded by Scots to educate Presbyterian ministers, whose religion demanded that they have a grounding in Greek and Latin. The most influential of these schools, Princeton University, was founded as the College of New Jersey in 1746. Scots also helped found nonsectarian institutions of higher education. James Blair, who came to the United States from Scotland in 1685, was the chief founder and the first president of William and Mary College (1693–1743). Joseph Caldwell helped establish the University of North Carolina, the nation's

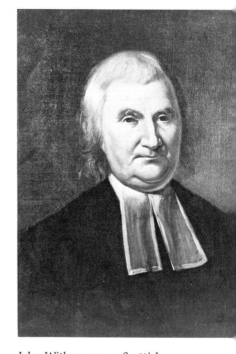

John Witherspoon, a Scottish-American clergyman, political leader, and educator, moved to the colonies in 1768 to become president of the College of New Jersey, a position he held until his death in 1794. Active in the politics of the emerging new nation, he was the only minister to sign the Declaration of Independence. Witherspoon also played a major role in organizing the Presbyterian church in the United States.

first public university, and became its first president in 1789. Scots also were involved in the founding of Dickinson College in New Jersey and Mercer College in Georgia.

The most accomplished Scottish-American religious leader, John Witherspoon, was a Presbyterian clergyman, the president of the College of New Jersey, and an influential politician. Born in Edinburgh in 1723, he was the child of a minister and descended from a long line of Calvinist clergymen. At the tender age of 13, Witherspoon entered Edinburgh University, receiving his master's degree 7 years later. He was ordained in 1745 and preached in Scotland until 1768. Early in his career he became a member of the Popular party (a faction within the Presbyterian church), lecturing against the liberal humanism of the Moderate party, which he felt was threatening to destroy traditional Presbyterian beliefs. A stern individual, his published works included *A Serious Treatise into the Nature and Effects of the Stage* (1757), which denounced the theater as excessively passionate. Despite his moral severity, he was wholly on the side of the people in matters of personal conscience, such as their right to select their own ministers. Witherspoon preached and lectured regularly on the subject of Presbyterian orthodoxy and denounced what he perceived to be increasing decadence in the church.

Witherspoon left Scotland in 1768 to assume the presidency of the College of New Jersey. In the first eight years of his tenure, the student body, faculty, and endowment increased dramatically. Witherspoon added the study of philosophy, French, oratory, and history to the curriculum, and he advocated courses that prepared students for public service. Witherspoon tutored James Madison and other leaders, endowing them with the values of the Scottish Enlightenment, perhaps most importantly the ideals of religious freedom and the separation of church and state.

A convert to Roman Catholicism, Elizabeth Ann Bayley Seton founded the Sisters of Charity of Saint Joseph in 1809, a religious order that established the model for the parochial school system in the United States. Seton, shown wearing the vestments of her order in this portrait, was the first native-born U.S. citizen to be named a saint.

In contrast to his immediate immersion in the religious and educational affairs of his new land, Witherspoon's involvement in American politics grew slowly. He was a county delegate, serving on committees of correspondence and in provincial conventions. His sermons and writings were tremendously influential in the period leading up to the war. In June 1776 he was selected as a delegate to the Continental Congress. Among his most significant acts in that body was a pivotal speech given on July 2, 1776, urging an immediate declaration of independence. The colonies, he said, were "not only ripe for the measure—but in danger of rotting for want of it."

A signer of the Declaration of Independence, Witherspoon served in Congress from 1776 to 1782, sitting on more than 100 committees, including the important Board of War and the Committee on Foreign Affairs. In the face of despair and fearfulness, he worked tirelessly and with courage. From 1782 until his death in 1794, he worked to rebuild the College of New Jersey from the setbacks it had suffered during the war. Reluctant to retreat entirely into the academic realm, he continued to serve sporadically in government and the church. Fittingly, he was chosen as the moderator of the very first General Assembly of the Presbyterian Church of the United States held in May 1789.

Another influential religious leader, Saint Elizabeth Ann Bayley Seton, was descended from a long line of Scots. A convert to Catholicism, Seton founded the Roman Catholic order of the Sisters of Charity in 1809 in Baltimore, Maryland. She was the first mother superior of the order. She also established a boarding school for girls from wealthy families and a day school for the poor in Emmitsburg, Maryland. The Sisters of Charity subsequently opened houses in Philadelphia in 1814 and New York in 1817. Mother Seton, as she was called, was one of the pioneers in the parochial school movement and was canonized in 1975.

Medicine

The Scots had a tremendous impact on North American medicine in the 18th century. In the period from 1740 to 1760, the Scottish universities—particularly Edinburgh and Glasgow—were in the forefront of medical science and education, far ahead of any European city. By the mid-18th century, the medical school at Edinburgh was commonly acknowledged as the best in the Western world. Those physicians trained at these splendid schools who later came to the United States settled throughout the colonies. Their influence can be discerned in many U.S. medical schools even today.

Among the eminent Scottish doctors who settled in Charleston, South Carolina, were John Lining and Lionel Chalmers. Lining came to the colonies around 1730, and unlike his U.S.-trained contemporaries, his education had included the study of literature, philosophy, and science in addition to medicine. Proof of the well-rounded nature of his interests is seen in the fact that he and Chalmers were early members of the Charlestown Library Society. Lining is best remembered for his pioneering work on yellow fever, then a devastating disease. His *Treatise on Yellow Fever* (1771) contained careful descriptions of the "symptoms, progress and chronology" of the disease, as well as precise meteorological observations (at the time, outbreaks of yellow fever were mistakenly thought to be triggered by the weather). Lining was also one of the first to conduct experiments on human metabolism. Lionel Chalmers arrived in the colonies in 1737, and like Lining he published works on fevers and the effects of weather on health. His *Essay on Fevers* was published in Charleston and London, and his two-volume work, *An Account of the Weather and Disease of South Carolina* (1776), was one of the finest general medical textbooks in the colonies.

Among the many Edinburgh University–trained physicians who settled in Virginia, James Craik is perhaps the best known. The son of a well-to-do landowner, Craik came to the colonies at age 20. He became a surgeon at the army fort in Winchester, Virginia, and soon was commissioned as a regimental surgeon. When Washington became commander in chief of the Virginia forces, Craik was named his chief medical officer. In 1777, Washington appointed Craik assistant physician general and because of his outstanding service Congress appointed him physician and surgeon of the army in 1781.

Craik and Washington were close friends, and the doctor often acted as the president's personal physician. On December 14, 1799, Craik was called to Washington's bedside at about 9:00 A.M. Craik diagnosed

Dr. James Craik (1730–1814) (second from left) attends to George Washington on his deathbed. Craik left Scotland for the colonies when he was 20 years old and later became a doctor in the Continental army. Washington appointed Craik as his chief medical officer, and Craik remained his physician and friend after the war.

Benjamin Rush (1745–1813) was one of the many North Americans who studied medicine in Scotland during the mid-18th century. Rush's subsequent work in education, social theory, politics, ethics, and religion exemplifies the Scottish values in which he was schooled. An important consequence of the exchange of medical knowledge between Scotland and North America was the influx of new social and political ideas such as the separation of church and state.

"acute laryngitis" and saw that little could be done. He bled the patient—a common practice at that time—and gave him medicines. The illness moved quickly, and the first president of the United States died at 10:00 P.M. Washington remembered Craik in his will in this way: "To my compatriot in arms, and old and intimate friend, Dr. Craik, I give my bureau (or, as the cabinet makers call it, tambour secretary), and the circular chair, an appendage of my study."

In the mid-18th century, a significant number of North Americans went to Scotland to study medicine, a trend that continued in increasing numbers to the end of the century. Of those born in North America who went to Scotland to study medicine, Benjamin Rush is the most acclaimed. Of English and Scottish descent, Rush was immersed in Scottish traditions and Presbyterian values. Raised in a liberal branch of the Presbyterian church, he attended Nottingham Academy (run by his uncle, a Scotch-Irish Presbyterian minister) and then the College of New Jersey. From there he began a medical apprenticeship and started classes at the new Medical College in Philadelphia (later part of the University of Pennsylvania).

Rush went to Edinburgh University in 1766, carrying letters of introduction from Benjamin Franklin, an ardent admirer of the Scottish universities. There, he finished his medical education and also studied literature, rhetoric, and natural and moral philosophy. An enthusiastic student, Rush was befriended by political, social, literary, and religious leaders in the city. Returning to the colonies in 1769, he built a thriving practice in Philadelphia and became a professor at the Medical College. Among his many books, *Medical Inquiries and Observations on the Diseases of the Mind* was the first psychiatry textbook written in the United States.

A man of enlightened and humane values, Rush's service in educational, social, and political affairs was staggering. He was surgeon general of the middle department of the Continental Army, a member of the Continental Congress, a signer of the Declaration of Independence, and a member of the Pennsylvania ratifying convention. He founded Dickinson College and the first antislavery society; was active in prison reform and the improement of the treatment of the insane; devised a plan for the establishment of public schools in Pennsylvania; and set up the first free medical dispensary in the United States.

When North Americans who completed their medical education in Scotland returned home, they settled on the East Coast and on the frontier. Many were from Philadelphia and returned to live there; it rapidly became the medical capital of the nation. The country's first medical college was established in Philadelphia, and the faculty boasted a number of Scottish-trained doctors. The nation's first general hospital, also in Philadelphia, was founded by Thomas Bond, who had studied under the Scottish doctor Alexander Hamilton and then at Edinburgh. Many Scottish-trained doctors and their students also settled in Boston and New York. Nearly all the medical personnel in the Continental army were either trained at Scottish universities or had been apprenticed under men who had been.

Scottish-born and Scottish-educated physicians in the United States were a small fraction of all practicing physicians there. But it is important to remember that of the roughly 3,500 people practicing medicine in 1775, only 350 or 400 had any formal training and only half of these had actual degrees. Most of the degree holders were educated in Scotland. Those who were either Scottish or trained in Scotland exercised influence and held positions of leadership substantially out of proportion to their number, founding two of the first medical schools in the United States and adding much to the improvement of medicine as a profession.

Edinburgh-trained men such as Benjamin Rush and John Morgan pioneered the integration of medical education into university programs. The earlier English model for medical training confined it entirely to the hospital. Scottish training in moral philosophy and the humanities led these men to the conviction that patients must be diagnosed and treated as whole people; that it is not only the body that must be healed but also the spirit and mind. Ultimately, the great contribution of the Scottish doctors was to give medicine a humane character beyond its technical precision.

Science and Industry

Many Scottish Americans have made impressive contributions to North American society in the field of science. Alexander Wilson, who immigrated to the

United States in 1794, was the first naturalist to study North American birds in their native habitats. Wilson prepared the first 7 volumes of *American Ornithology* (1808–13), which contain color illustrations and the life histories of 268 species of birds. The writings of another Scottish-American naturalist, John Muir, contributed to the establishment of the Yosemite and Sequoia national parks and the Sierra National Forest.

Scottish-American inventors have also been recognized for their contributions to society. Samuel Colt invented the first revolving-breech pistol, or revolver. He built a large arms factory in Hartford, Connecticut, to mass-produce the weapons. Colt also invented a remote-control naval mine and an underwater telegraph cable. Alexander Graham Bell immigrated with his family to Ontario, Canada, in 1870. With his father, Bell conducted research in the field of speech and deafness. He became a professor of vocal physiology at Boston University, where he tried to develop a harmonic telegraph that would transmit several telegraphic messages over the same line. In 1875, he discovered the principles that made the telephone possible and

In 1871, Alexander Graham Bell (1847–1922) (top right) poses with the faculty and students of the Boston School for the Deaf. Through research related to his work with deaf children, Bell discovered the underlying principles of the telephone. He was granted a patent for the telephone in 1876 and received 29 other patents involving telephonic communication and instruction of the deaf.

Wearing a resplendent kilt, Forbes *magazine publisher Malcolm Forbes (1919–90) and Elizabeth Taylor are photographed during a 1987 gala held at the Forbes estate to celebrate the magazine's 70th anniversary. Scottish immigrant Bertie Forbes, Malcolm's father, founded the magazine in 1917 to help improve the quality of corporate management.*

received the first patent on the telephone one year later. He also invented a number of other devices, including a submarine chaser and the tetrahedral (four-faced) kite.

Perhaps the best-known inventor of partly Scottish descent is Thomas Alva Edison, whose maternal grandparents were Scottish. Despite having completed only three months of formal education, Edison became one of the world's most celebrated and productive inventors. At 21, he patented his first major invention, a stock ticker for printing stock-exchange quotations. Edison soon established the largest private laboratory in the world in Menlo Park, New Jersey, and began directing a team of scientists and engineers in a wide range of projects. In the 1870s, Edison developed the phonograph and the first practical light bulb, perhaps his greatest triumph. He installed the first large central power station in New York City in 1882. Edison's other inventions include the alkaline storage battery, the carbon microphone, and the movie projector.

Scottish Americans have had a profound effect on business and industry in the United States. The Scots who came to the United States and Canada in the 19th and 20th centuries were mostly laborers, farmers, or skilled artisans. Overwhelming numbers of them found work in industry, and their achievements tended to be in business, industrial invention, and engineering. The financial success of Andrew Carnegie, for example, virtually paralleled the industrial history of the United States during his lifetime. In an attempt to provide a forum to raise the standards of corporate responsibility to investors, Scotsman Bertie Charles Forbes founded *Forbes* magazine in 1917. The business-oriented magazine profiles leaders in industry and seeks to reveal and explain the quality and impact of management policies on business performance. Forbes's son Malcolm became publisher of the magazine in 1957.

The Arts

Scottish-American artists have also enriched the culture of North America. Gilbert Charles Stuart (1755–1828), whose parents were Scots, was the foremost portrait painter of his day. He painted several penetrating portraits of Washington, as well as outstanding ones of John Adams, John Quincy Adams, Thomas Jefferson, James Madison, and John Jacob Astor, among others. Alexander Hay Ritchie, who was born in Scotland, received wide acclaim for his paintings *Death of Lincoln*

Scottish-American sculptor and painter Alexander Calder (1898–1976) assembles one of his characteristic mobiles in his studio in 1966.

and *Washington and His Generals*. Duncan Phyfe, famed cabinetmaker and furniture designer, was born in Loch Fannich and moved to the United States in 1783. Phyfe's furniture is characterized by its grace and delicate artistic beauty. Alexander Calder, one of the best-known sculptors of the 20th century, came from a long line of Scots. Calder received much acclaim for his mobiles constructed of metal and wire. His father, Stirling, and his grandfather, Alexander Milne Calder, were also sculptors; the latter is best known for his statue of William Penn that sits atop Philadelphia's City Hall.

The first newspaper printed in North America, *The Boston News-Letter*, was published by a Scot, John Campbell, who was also a bookseller and a postmaster. Lawyer, soldier, and novelist Lew Wallace was of Scottish descent. *Ben-Hur* (1880) is the best known of his many novels. Pulitzer Prize–winning reporter James Reston, Sr., was born in Scotland on November 3, 1909, and moved to the United States with his family at the age of one. From 1934 to 1939, Reston worked as a reporter for the Associated Press in its New York and London bureaus. Reston joined the *New York Times* in 1939, serving as the newspaper's chief Washington correspondent (1953–64) and as a daily columnist from 1974 until his retirement in 1989.

The Ingersoll Bagpipe Band from Ingersoll, Canada, performs during the Grandfather Mountain Highland Games. Many Scottish Americans maintain a strong affection for their ancestry.

THREE CENTURIES
OF SCOTS IN
NORTH AMERICA

More than most other immigrant groups that have
settled in North America, the Scots have acquired a
romantic and largely mythological history. They have
been idealized and credited with sweeping cultural
achievements that were actually the work of many
peoples working together. Nonetheless, what the Scots
actually did contribute to North America—as individuals and as a group—is worthwhile and ad-
mirable. John Witherspoon, for example, brought
critical ideas about the separation of church and state
and about religious toleration to North America. He
taught these ideals of the Scottish Enlightenment at
Princeton and preached them from his pulpit. Perhaps
most important, he instilled them in James Madison and
thereby ensured that they would one day be fixed in the
First Amendment to the Constitution.

The Scottish Presbyterians were not, as is so often claimed, inherently egalitarian and thereby responsible for the democratic revolution. In fact, their faith is oligarchic (controlled by a few leaders), and their political loyalties before and during the American Revolution did much to hinder the cause of the patriots. However, Scottish Presbyterianism brought about other developments in North American culture. Its emphasis on a rigorously educated clergy led to the founding of a number of academies and colleges, including Princeton University. Graduates of these schools were among the initiators of the first great religious revival in America, the Great Awakening, which swept the colonies in the 1740s. The Presbyterian sense of responsibility and seriousness charged Scottish merchants with the purposefulness to succeed. The lack of opportunities in Scotland motivated immigrants who ventured to North America to work hard and to save and invest their money. The enthusiastic Scots provided much of the mercantile energy necessary for the industrialization of the United States in the 19th century. Their pragmatism and eagerness for innovation stand out notably in individuals such as Alexander Graham Bell. Finally, Presbyterianism's emphasis on public service caused many to seek public office or, like Andrew Carnegie, to undertake invaluable philanthropic work.

The Future

Although the Scots have never been a large ethnic group within the total North American population, their percentage has grown smaller even as their numbers have increased. For example, approximately 6 percent of the population of the United States in 1790 was of Scottish origin. Despite the massive migrations of the 19th century, this percentage diminished to 3.1 by 1850. In 1900, Scots totaled 2.4 percent of the nation's population and in 1920, 2.1 percent. Though the number of people of Scottish birth in the United States reached

899,592 in 1930, they represented a mere 2.5 percent of the whole population. In 1980, only about 142,000 foreign-born Scots resided in the United States, representing less than 1 percent of the nation's population.

Though the Scots have come to be just one more ethnic group in the vast mélange of North American society, it is interesting to note that affection for Scottish ancestry seems only to increase. People flock to Highland Games and clan gatherings. Even those of only partial Scottish descent are proud to display and celebrate their heritage.

At the Highland Games held annually at Grandfather Mountain, North Carolina, a contender in the hammer throw competition heaves the 22-pound object with all his might. Showing pride in their heritage, Scottish Americans flock to Highland Games and clan gatherings held throughout the United States and Canada.

FURTHER READING

Adam, Margaret I. "The Highland Emigration of 1770." *The Scottish Historical Review*, vol. 16. Glasgow: James MacLehose & Sons, 1919.

Boswell, James. *Boswell's Life of Johnson. Vol. 5: Journal of a Tour to the Hebrides with Samuel Johnson, LL.D.* 2nd ed. Edited by George Birkbeck Hill and L. F. Powell. London: Oxford University Press, 1964.

Brownlee, Robert. *An American Odyssey.* Fayetteville: University of Arkansas Press, 1986.

Bumsted, J. M. *The People's Clearance: Highland Emigration to British North America, 1770–1815.* Edinburgh: Edinburgh University Press, 1982.

Erikson, Charlotte. *The Invisible Immigrants: The Adaptation of English and Scottish Immigrants in Nineteenth Century America.* London: Weidenfeld & Nicholson, 1972.

Fischer, David Hackett. *Albion's Seed: Four British Folkways in America.* New York: Oxford University Press, 1989.

Galbraith, John Kenneth. *The Scotch.* 2nd ed. Boston: Houghton Mifflin, 1985.

Graham, Ian Charles Cargill. *Colonists from Scotland: Emigration to North America, 1707–1783.* Ithaca: Cornell University Press, 1956.

Kailyn, Bernard. *Voyagers to the West.* New York: Knopf, 1986.

Lehmann, William C. *Scottish and Scotch-Irish Contributions to Early American Life and Culture.* Port Washington, NY: National University Publications/Kenmkat Press, 1978.

Mackie, J. D. *A History of Scotland.* 2nd ed. Harmondsworth, Middlesex, England: Penguin Books, 1987.

Morison, Samuel Eliot, Henry Steele Commager, and William E. Leuchtenburg. *The Growth of the American Republic.* 7th ed. New York: Oxford University Press, 1980.

INDEX

CATHERINE AMAN is an educator and freelance writer based in New York City. She received an A.B. in American history from Brown University.

DANIEL PATRICK MOYNIHAN is the senior United States senator from New York. He is also the only person in American history to serve in the cabinets or subcabinets of four successive presidents—Kennedy, Johnson, Nixon, and Ford. Formerly a professor of government at Harvard University, he has written and edited many books, including *Beyond the Melting Pot*, *Ethnicity: Theory and Experience* (both with Nathan Glazer), *Loyalties*, and *Family and Nation*.

PICTURE CREDITS

Alexandria Convention and Visitors Bureau: pp. 53 (bottom), 55, 56; AP/Wide World Photos: pp. 90, 93; The Bettmann Archive: pp. 28, 29, 33, 38, 41, 70, 84, 87, 89; Courtesy of the British Tourist Authority: pp. 20, 22; Delco Scottish Games, Inc.: p. 53 (top); Glasgow Collection, Mitchell Library: pp. 67, 68; Courtesy the Henry Francis Du Pont Winterthur Museum: p. 96; Courtesy of Independence National Historical Park, National Park Service: p. 91; Library of Congress: pp. 31, 36, 69, 73, 80, 85; M & M Karolik Fund, courtesy Museum of Fine Arts, Boston: p. 95; Foto Marburg/Art Resource, NY: p. 24; Hugh Morton: pp. 49, 52, 104–5, 107; Muscarelle Museum of Art, College of William and Mary in Virginia: p. 34; National Archives of Canada: p. 75 (neg. #PA-41429); National Galleries of Scotland, Hole: *St. Columba Preaching to the Picts*: p. 25; National Galleries of Scotland, Wilkie: *Distraining for Rent*: p. 65; National Galleries of Scotland, Wright: *Lord Mungo Murray*: p. 18; National Park Service, Statue of Liberty National Monument: p. 99; Thomas Nichols: p. 54; Notman Photographic Archives, McCord Museum of Canadian History: cover, pp. 12–13, 15, 16, 57; Nova Scotia Museum, Halifax: p. 44; Perls Galleries, New York: p. 102; Picture Collection, the Branch Libraries, The New York Public Library: p. 26; The Presbyterian Church (U.S.)'s Department of History: pp. 60, 61; The Scottish Ethnological Archive, National Museums of Scotland: pp. 62–63, 76; James & Luola Sprunt, Sprunt Collection, Special Collections Department, Duke University Library, Durham, NC: pp. 78–79; Katrina Thomas: pp. 50, 51; Reproduced by permission of the Trustees of the National Library of Scotland: p. 42; UPI/Bettmann Archive: p. 100; Picture by A. Vienneau, courtesy of the New-York Historical Society, New York City: p. 47